The Story of the War

in

South Africa

1899–1900

Titles in The West Point Military Library

BARNARD, *Military Schools and Courses of Instruction in the Science and Art of War* (1872).
BIGELOW, *The Principles of Strategy. Illustrated Mainly from American Campaigns*, 2nd ed. (1894).
BIRKHIMER, *Historical Sketch of the Organization, Administration, Matériel and Tactics of the Artillery, United States Army* (1884).
BRACKETT, *History of the United States Cavalry to 1863* (1865).
FEUQUIERES, *Memoirs Historical and Military: Containing a Distinct View of All the Considerable States of Europe* (1735-1736). 2 vols.
HALLECK, *Elements of Military Art and Science* (1846).
HAMLEY, *The Story of the Campaign of Sebastopol, Written in the Camp* (1855).
HOYT, *Practical Instructions for Military Officers* (1811).
JAMES, *A New and Enlarged Military Dictionary, in French and English* (1810). 2 vols.
JOMINI, *Summary of the Art of War* (1854).
LLOYD, *The History of the Late War in Germany, Between the King of Prussia, and the Empress of Germany and Her Allies* (1781). 3 vols.
MAC DONALD, *Rules and Regulations for the Field Exercise and Manoeuvres of the French Infantry*, 2nd ed. (1806). 2 vols.
MAHAN, *The Story of the War in South Africa, 1899-1900 (1900).*
MAHAN, *A Complete Treatise on Field Fortification* (1836).
MALLESON, *The Battle-fields of Germany, from the Outbreak of the Thirty-Years War to the Battle of Blenheim* (1884).
MARMONT, *The Spirit of Military Institutions* (1864).
MITCHELL, *The Life of Wallenstein, Duke of Friedland* (1837).
MURRAY (ed.), *The Letters and Dispatches of John Churchill, First Duke of Marlborough, from 1702 to 1712* (1845). 5 vols.
The Officer's Manual in the Field; or, a Series of Military Plans, Representing the Principal Operations of a Campaign, 2nd ed. (1800).
PRUSSIA, Kriegsministerium, *Regulations for the Prussian Cavalry* (1757).
PRUSSIA, Kriegsministerium, *Regulations for the Prussian Infantry* (1759).
SCHELIHA, *A Treatise on Coast-Defense* (1868).
SCHMIDT, *Instructions for the Training, Employment, and Leading of Cavalry* (1881).
SCOTT, *Military Dictionary* (1862).
TOUSARD, *American Artillerist's Companion, or Elements of Artillery* (1809). 3 vols.
TURNER, *Pallas Armata. Military Essays of the Ancient Grecian, Roman, and Modern Art of War* (1683).
U.S. Military Academy, West Point, *The Centennial of the United States Military Academy at West Point, New York, 1802-1902* (1904). 2 vols.
U.S. War Department, *Instruction for Field Artillery* (1861).
UPTON, *The Armies of Asia and Europe* (1878).
UPTON, *Infantry Tactics, Double and Single Rank Adapted to American Topography and Improved Fire-arms*, rev. ed. (1874).
UPTON, *The Military Policy of the United States* (1904).
VERDY DU VERNOIS, *A Tactical Study, Based on the Battle of Custozza, 24th of June, 1866* (1894).
VERDY DU VERNOIS, *With the Royal Headquarters in 1870-71* (1897).
VIELE, *Handbook for Active Service* (1861).
WAGNER, *The Campaign of Königgrätz, a Study of the Austro-Prussian Conflict in the Light of the American Civil War* (1889).

CAPTAIN ALFRED T. MAHAN,

U.S.N.; D.C.L.

The

Story of the War in South Africa

1899–1900

By

Captain A. T. Mahan, U.S.N.

With Map and Portrait of the Author

GREENWOOD PRESS, PUBLISHERS
NEW YORK

Originally published in 1900 by
Sampson, Low, Marston and Company

First Greenwood Reprinting, 1968

Library of Congress Catalogue Card Number: 68-54796

PRINTED IN THE UNITED STATES OF AMERICA

CONTENTS

CHAPTER VII

CHAPTER VIII

THE

SOUTH AFRICAN WAR

CHAPTER I

THE THEATRE OF THE WAR

THE war in South Africa has been no exception to the general rule that the origin of current events is to be sought in the history of the past, and their present course to be understood by an appreciation of existing conditions, which decisively control it. This is especially true of the matter here before us; because the southern extreme of Africa, like to that of the American continent, has heretofore lain far outside of the common interest, and therefore of the accurate knowledge, of mankind at large. The Cape of Good Hope and Cape Horn, in themselves remote, tempestuous, and comparatively unproductive regions, for centuries derived importance merely from the fact that by those ways alone the European world found access to the shores of the Pacific and Indian Oceans. The application of steam to ocean navigation, and the opening of the Suez Canal, have greatly modified conditions, by diverting travel from the two Capes to the Canal and to the Straits of Magellan. It is only within a very few years that South Africa, thus diminished in consequence as a station upon a leading commercial highway, has received compensation by the discovery of great mineral wealth.

Thus separated from the rest of the world, by lack of intrinsic value as a region producing materials necessary to the common good, the isolation of South Africa was further increased by physical conditions, which not only retarded colonisation and development, but powerfully affected the character and the mutual relations of the European settlers. Portuguese mariners, after more than half a century of painful groping downward along the West African coast in search of a sea route to India that vague tradition asserted could there be found, in 1486 rounded the Cape of Good Hope, which then received the despondent name of the Cape of Storms from its first discoverer, Bartholomew Diaz.

Vasco da Gama, following him in 1497, gave to it its present auspicious title, which was to him of sound augury; for he then passed on to explore the East coast and to find the long-desired Indies. It was, however, the latter which constituted the Portuguese goal. Africa was to them primarily the half-way house, where to refresh their ships on the long voyage to Hindustan, which then took near a year to complete. For this purpose they established themselves on the island of Mozambique, and gradually took possession of the country to this day known as Portuguese East Africa.

From that far back settlement, Delagoa Bay, near the southern border, is now a thorn in the side of the British invasion; a port with which they are not at war, and therefore cannot seize or blockade, but which, through the supplies that thence reach the otherwise isolated Transvaal, contributes powerfully to support the defence.

Upon the heels of the Portuguese followed the Dutch, aiming like them at the Far East, more especially at what were then comprehensively called the Spice Islands — the Moluccas. They also felt the need of a half-way station. For this the Cape of Good Hope, with the adjacent bays—Table Bay and False Bay—presented advantages; for though not perfectly safe anchorages at all seasons, the voyage to the islands is more expeditiously and healthfully made by starting from, and keeping in, a far southern latitude, than by proceeding along the East African coast.

In 1652 the Dutch settled at the Cape, and gradually extended their holding to the eastward as far as the Great Fish River. A generation later, in 1686, the population received an accession of French Protestant refugees, leaving their country upon the revocation of the Edict of Nantes. From these descended the late General Joubert, Commander-in-Chief of the Transvaal forces at the opening of hostilities. The administration of the colony by the Dutch East India Company being both arbitrary and meddlesome, some of the more independent spirits withdrew from the coast and moved inland, behind the difficult mountain ranges that separate the narrow strip of sea-coast from the high table-lands of the interior.

In 1795 local dissatisfaction and the spread of French revolutionary principles led to a revolt of the colonists, and Holland passing at that time into alliance with France, the Cape was seized by a British naval and military expedition. At the Peace of Amiens in 1802 it was restored to Holland; but in the next war it was again taken by the British, in 1806, and at the Peace of 1814 was confirmed in their possession.

The population remained Dutch in blood and in tradition; but subsequent accessions of English immigrants have established in Cape Colony itself an approach to equilibrium between the two races, to which has also contributed a series of emigrations to the interior by the Dutch farmers, dissatisfied with various incidents of British rule. Into the merits of these differences we have neither space nor occasion to go.

In 1836, immediately prior to the largest of these movements, known as the Great Trek, the British Government, by Act, extended its claim of control over all South Africa, south of 25°, the latitude of Delagoa Bay; and the Boer emigrants were warned that in entering that region they remained under British authority, unless they passed on into the Portuguese dominion. From this Trek resulted directly, in the course of years, the two Boer states, the Orange Free State and the South African Republic (commonly called the Transvaal); and also, indirectly, the easternmost British colony in South Africa, Natal, in which the English element is decisively preponderant.

The mention of this migration leads naturally and immediately to a summary of the physical conditions of the country, by which, as well as by derivation of blood, the apartness of the two races has been emphasized. Between the narrow margin of land belonging, as it were, to the sea, and the high interior plateau, there runs from the extreme west of the British dominions a chain of lofty mountains, parallel, roughly, to the coastline, and terminating only when abreast of Delagoa Bay. These reach an elevation of from six to eight thousand feet, and in places on the border between Natal and Basutoland heights of eleven thousand are attained. On the side toward the sea the ascent is comparatively rapid and difficult, though often broken into precipitous terraces. Inland the descent is less, and more regular, issuing in a plateau from three to five thousand feet above the sea, and presenting almost throughout a comparatively level or undulating surface that offers no serious difficulty to transit.

The territory of the Orange Free State and of the Transvaal lies wholly within this tableland. In this region, and throughout Africa south of 25°, there are river beds, but no navigable rivers. The country is generally treeless, and there is a great deficiency of steady natural water supply. During the rainy season, from October to March, the naked ground fails to retard the running off of the waters, which therefore escape rapidly by the rivers, swelling them to momentary torrents that quickly and fruitlessly subside. During the long dry season the exposed herbage dries to the roots.

From these conditions it results that not only is agriculture generally impracticable, economically, but that cattle and sheep, the chief wealth of the Boer farmers, require an unusual proportion of ground per head for pasture; and the mobility of bodies of horsemen, expecting to subsist their beasts upon local pasturage, is greatly affected by the seasons—an important military consideration. The large holdings introduce large spaces between the holders, who dwell therefore alone, each man with his family. So it has come to pass that the descendants of one of the most mercantile and gregarious of races, whose artists have won some of their chiefest triumphs in depicting the joyous episodes of crowded social life, have, through calling and environment, become lovers of solitude, austere, self-dependent, disposed rather to repel than to seek their kind.

The same conditions, unfavourable to the aggregation of people into towns or villages, have interfered with the development of lines of travel, roads and cross-roads, which not only facilitate but define movement; and as the face of the country, readily traversable in all directions, does not compel roads to take a particular direction to avoid obstacles, it has come to pass that the seat of war within the territory of the two Boer states has, like the ocean, and for the same reasons, few strategic points either natural or artificial.

The determining natural military features in South Africa are the seaports, upon possession of which depends Great Britain's landing her forces, and the mountain ranges, the passes of which, as in all such regions, are of the utmost strategic value. It has been said that the Boers' original plan of campaign was to force the British out of Natal, thus closing access by Durban from the sea, and at the same time to seize the pass back of Cape Town known as Hex River. If successful, the eastern flank of the Boer frontier would have been secured against British landing by the occupation of Durban, while advance from Cape Town, against the other extremity, would have involved a front attack upon a strong position in a difficult mountain defile.

These movements, accurate in conception, were probably in any case too developed for the Boer numbers, and were definitively foiled by the British grip upon Ladysmith and Kimberley. Advance was too hazardous, leaving in the rear such forces, unchecked, upon the flank of the lines of communication.

To these two extremes, or flanks, of the Boer frontier, correspond on the British side the ports of Cape Town and Durban, which may be said to mark the western and eastern limits of the field of military operations in the war. They are the chief sea-ports on the South African coast, which by nature is singularly deficient in good and safe anchorages. The advantages of these two, artificially improved, and combined with the relatively open and productive region immediately behind them, have made them the starting-points of the principal railroad lines by which, through the sea, the interior is linked to the outer world.

The general direction of these roads is determined, as always, by the principal objects of traffic or other interests. Thus the line from Cape Town, ascending by a winding course through the mountains in the rear, pushes its way north to Kimberley, where are the great diamond fields, and thence on, by way of Mafeking, to the territory of the British South African Company—now known as Rhodesia. This lies north of the Transvaal, and, like it, is separated from the sea by the Portuguese dominion, having, however, by treaty a right of military way through the latter by the port of Beira; of which right use is now being made.

In the northern part of its course, which at present ends at Buluwayo, this road is as yet rather political than economical in its importance, joining the British entrance at the sea to the as yet little developed regions of the distant interior. At a point called De Aar Junction, five hundred miles from Cape Town, a principal branch is thrown off to the eastward to Bloemfontein, the capital of the Orange Free State, whence it continues on to Johannesburg, the great industrial centre of the Gold Fields, and to Pretoria, the capital of the Transvaal. A glance along this stretch of road will show that between De Aar and Bloemfontein it receives three tributary routes from three different points of the sea-coast—Port Elizabeth, Port Alfred, and East London—the whole system concentrating some sixty miles before Bloemfontein, at Springfontein, which thus becomes a central depot fed by four convergent, but, in their origin, independent streams of supply; an administrative condition always conducive to security and to convenience. This instance also illustrates the capital importance—especially in a military point of view—of a place where meet several roads from the permanent base of operations, which in the case of the British interior campaign is the sea. The fall of Springfontein would close every avenue of supply by rail; but a blow at any one of the four lines which concentrate there does not necessarily affect the others. Holding across-roads in fact exemplifies the homely phrase of killing two birds with one stone.

Beyond Springfontein the straightness of the line sufficiently testifies to the easy practicability of the country it traverses. Upon this railroad system depend the supplies of the British army, which presents in both men and animals a concentrated mass of life heretofore unknown to the territory in which it is moving, and where, from previous conditions of population and development, necessary resources of every kind are deficient. This system constitutes the main chain of communications, as the term is understood in war; by it chiefly, for much of the distance wholly, must come all the ammunition, most of the food, and not improbably at times a good deal of the water drunk during the dry season, which fortunately, from this point of view, is also that of cooler weather.

The difficulty of reinforcing railway carriage by any other system of road transportation is greatly increased by the local horse-sickness, from which three-fourths of the horses exposed to it die. Reliance for that purpose, therefore, must be upon the ox-wagon, which for this reason, and owing to the open level character of the country, has in the past played a leading part in the South African migrations.

The main and subsidiary railroads thus summarized should, from the point of view of our subject, be considered as one, contributory to the advance of the British army over a substantially even country, which opposes few natural obstacles to such a movement, though here and there "accidents of the ground"—a range of hills, or a dry river-bed, as at Paardeberg—may facilitate opposition by a military force. The system receives no further support until Johannesburg is reached. There the railroad from Durban comes in, and, if its carrying capacity were adequate, which is doubtful, would enable the chief base of operations and main line of communications to be shifted to the nearer locality, retaining the Cape road only as secondary.

The advantage to the British of the line of invasion from Cape Town is that it crosses the mountains, which separate the coast district from the inland plateau, at such a distance from the enemy's frontier that it is impossible for the latter to offer serious resistance before the comparatively easy rolling country has been reached. It was for this reason that the decision of the Orange Free State to join in the war, while it added to the numerical resistance to be encountered by the British, had for them the compensating advantage that it removed the necessity of forcing their way over the difficult mountain ranges which separate Natal from the Transvaal.

With the power of Great Britain to bring

into the field a great superiority of numbers, it is at least open to argument that the Free State, by ceasing to be neutral, relieved the enemy of a difficulty greater than that which its hostility introduced. It was for these reasons that the original British plan, as generally understood, was to make the main invasion along this line. The danger of Ladysmith, it is commonly and with probability believed, caused the momentary abandonment of this purpose. Whether the change was at the moment correct in principle or not, it is evident that Lord Roberts has reverted to the first intention; a course which enforces its accuracy with all the weight of his well-earned great renown.

The other railroad system of direct importance to the military operations of the present war is the single Natal line, from Durban to Johannesburg and Pretoria, which at Ladysmith throws off a branch to the westward, crossing the mountains to Bethlehem in the Free State, and there ends, over sixty miles from the road between Bloemfontein and Pretoria. The Natal road, having been opened as lately as 1895, may be considered the child of the Gold Fields; prior to the discovery of which, indeed, there were in the Transvaal neither products nor consumers enough to give commercial value to a railroad.

The Cape Town line reached Pretoria only in 1892, and it is still characteristic of all the lines that there is but little local traffic, either freight or passenger; the roads exist as means whereby the function of communication, so far discharged by the sea, is prolonged from the coast to the interior of the continent.

It is not the least noteworthy in the incidents of commercial and mechanical energy, by which foreign hands have developed the Transvaal from a poor to a wealthy state, that "all the heavy machinery, the timber, the corrugated iron with which the works and men's houses are constructed, and nearly every requirement of work and life, had to be brought for over three hundred miles upon ox-wagons, the country itself supplying scarcely anything, and even to this day (1897) wheat being brought from Australia." *

* Younghusband's "South Africa of To-day." Second Edition, 1899.

Regarded as a source of supply, especially of military supply, the demands of which are more urgent than those of common life, as its needs and dangers are more imminent, the Natal railroad, though much shorter in distance to the probable scenes of operations, labours under two disadvantages. The port of Durban is not under all circumstances safe for large vessels to enter, and there is therefore in the facilities for landing goods an inferiority to Cape Town. The country, too, is more difficult, the obstacles to movement, which also favour defence, increasing as the frontier is approached, and culminating on the borders of the Free State and the Transvaal. Being thus nearer, the latter are here better able to concentrate and sustain opposition than they are on the western flank.

"The mountains which on the edge of Basutoland rise to a height of ten thousand feet," writes Mr. Bryce, "break down toward Natal in tremendous precipices. Near Ladysmith the frontier of the Orange Free State coincides with a high watershed, crossed by only a few passes."* Where this boundary

* "Impressions of South Africa." Third Edition, p. 291.

between Natal and the Free State ends, that of the Transvaal begins, and soon after turns sharply to the southward, the new direction forming with the old a very acute angle, with apex to the north. Here, just within the territory of Natal, is Majuba Hill, whose name has been in the mouths of all men, and Laing's Nek, less familiarly known. The narrow neck of rugged country embraced between the legs of this angle is about sixty miles long, from Majuba to Glencoe. Recent events have familiarised to us many of the names along this line of rail — Glencoe, Dundee (the terminus of a short branch), Colenso, Estcourt, and Ladysmith itself; while the winding character of the track, as mapped, compared with the Free State road, sufficiently indicates the character of the country, in which obstacles have to be circumvented as well as overcome. The grade is in places as high as one in thirty, though that is being reduced; but one in forty is common. Pietermaritzburg, the capital, fifty miles from Durban in a straight line, is 2,200 feet above the sea. Three hundred miles from its starting-point the road reaches an elevation of over five thousand feet, at Laing's Nek, through which it passes by a tunnel.

A topographical map of the country shows upon examination that the mountain range, which forms the western boundary of Natal toward Basutoland and the Orange Free State, and has a general north and south direction parallel to the railroad, throws off to the eastward spurs which, to repeat Mr. Bryce's expression, "break down in tremendous precipices," forming a succession of terraces. The gorges between these determine the direction of the river-beds whereby the rainfall pours down to the sea; and the general easterly course thus imparted is maintained and continued by the lie of the valleys, separating the successive hills through which the territory of Natal gradually rises to the northward. These various streams find their way sooner or later to the Tugela, itself one of the many, but which carries its own name until it reaches the Indian Ocean, some fifty miles north-east of Durban.

Of these watercourses, the Tugela, which the road crosses at Colenso, and the Mooi, some fifty miles south, have been most often mentioned. Another tributary called the Klip flows through the camp at Ladysmith. The channels which these streams have cut for themselves in time of torrent are both steep-banked and deep. They are therefore among those accidents of the ground which, duly improved, can seriously affect military operations. The destruction of a bridge impedes the transport of troops and supplies; a sudden freshet, occurring in the midst of an extensive movement, may imperil an army by sundering its forces; while of the utility of such natural trenches to the purposes of shelter and of defence, of awaiting attack, or resisting an advance, both the Tugela and Paardeberg have given recent striking illustration.

As a general rule such conditions favour the defence relatively to the offence; the former, remaining comparatively motionless, is shielded by obstacles, to surmount which the assailant must expose himself in the open. Thus they compensate for inferior numbers, which is usually the condition of the defence; and they conduce to delay, ever a leading object in defensive warfare. Consequently, in the present hostilities they have helped the Boers. It may be added that their influence is most felt when the armies are face to face, or at least in touch. Hence their existence near the scene of probable conflict, as in Natal, is a matter of more concern to the invader than when, as upon the Cape extreme of the scene of war, they are found beyond the range to which the defendant can safely extend his operations.

These successive watercourses indicate natural lines of defence, stronger or weaker according to their individual distinctive features. As the railroad, in its progress north, draws near the mountains in the neck of Natal, the streams show smaller volume and less developed channels. This comes from their having there a shorter course and descending from heights which, though still considerable, are decidedly lower. But, while the streams become less conspicuous as obstacles, the ground toward the northward frontier is more broken and irregular, presenting numerous scattered hills, sometimes isolated, sometimes in small ranges or groups, which to a trained military skill afford positions too threatening to be disregarded, and yet which cannot be carried without heavy loss. This characteristic is observable in the neighbourhood of Glencoe, Dundee, and Ladysmith, and, as will be seen, exercised a determinative influence upon the fighting.

In the extreme north a similar condition is emphasized conspicuously at Majuba Hill and the surrounding country, which, however, and perhaps for that very reason, seem unlikely to play much of a part in the war now current.

Before proceeding to the narrative of the hostilities which, so far as events of decisive interest are concerned, began in Natal, it is desirable to note one broad topographical feature distinguishing the region to which, in its eastern development, the war has been confined. From the capital, Pietermaritzburg, the railroad ascends rapidly, so that in twenty-five miles it has risen from 2,200 to 4,800 feet, after which it begins again to go down, till fifty miles further, at Estcourt — the most southern of the stations prominently named in the narratives of the war—the elevation is 3,800 feet. Thence, till near Glencoe and

Dundee, there is an extensive area of comparative depression, rarely itself higher than 3,500 feet, but on the western side skirted by the precipitous spurs of the border mountains, close to which the railroad passes.

This district may be called the valley of the Tugela; for all the streams tend to the latter, which finds its own bed in a broad belt of ground, trending to the eastward, where the surface sinks to less than 3,000 feet. Ladysmith itself, important not only as a railroad crossing and military depot, but now also historically, on account of the operations centring around it, is at a height of 3,300. Beyond it the country, though often rough in detail, is gently rolling in general contour till near Glencoe, where the road climbs eight hundred feet in ten miles. From Glencoe a branch runs five miles east to Dundee, the site of extensive collieries, upon which Natal largely depends for fuel.

The railroad from Ladysmith to Glencoe passes therefore through a district the nature of which is favourable to rapid advance or retreat of mounted men, as the Boer forces chiefly are, and which at the same time is marked by frequent and steep detached elevations, adapted for defensive positions hastily assumed. These conditions, with the nearness of the declivities of the western mountains, and the proximity of the enemy's frontier, behind which movements of troops would be "curtained"—to use a graphic military metaphor—gave the Boers particular facilities for striking unexpectedly the railroad between Ladysmith and Glencoe, upon which, in defect of other transportation, the two British posts must depend for communication between themselves, and with their base on the sea.

Further to the south, movements of the same kind would be decisively more difficult. Not only would the Boers there be further from their base, and the British nearer theirs, but the country is less favourable to rapid horse movements, the line of the rail is contracted by lofty and continuous ranges of hills, the space between which gives but a narrow front to be covered by a defence, and the river beds, as already said, are broader and deeper; notably, of course, the Tugela. Moreover, not only are the mountains on the western frontier higher and more difficult as one goes south, they are also more remote; and, south of Colenso, form the boundary of Basutoland, upon which the Boers could not intrude without arousing armed resistance by the blacks. All these conditions are more favourable to a pure defensive attitude, which was that imposed at the outset upon the British, because they were then numerically the weaker party.

And here at once must be made a distinction, which for intelligent comprehension it is essential to keep in mind. Putting entirely to one side all question of the merits of the quarrel—of its right or its wrong—it must be steadily remembered that, although the comparative aggregate strength of the two parties placed the Boers from the first on the defensive in the general sense, they were at the beginning of hostilities decisively superior in local force, and would so remain until sufficient reinforcements from Great Britain should arrive to turn the scale. Under such circumstances, correct military principle — and the Boers have had good advisers—imperatively dictates that the belligerent so situated must at once assume an active offensive. By rapid and energetic movement, while the opponent's forces are still separated, every advantage must be seized to destroy hostile detachments within reach, and to establish one's own front as far in advance of the great national interests, as it can be reasonably hoped to maintain it with communications unbroken. The line thus occupied must rest upon positions so chosen that by their strength, natural and developed, it shall be possible, when offence has to be exchanged for defensive warfare, to impose to the utmost upon the invader both delay and loss; for delay and loss mean lessening power, and only by causing such diminution, greater relatively than his own, can the weaker hope eventually to reverse the odds and win the game.

To this end, therefore, the Boers with sound military judgment at once devoted themselves; and it is very likely that the surmise before quoted was correct—in naming the Hex River Pass and Durban as their ultimate objectives, to be reached by a swift advance. The latter was certainly not an unreasonable hope, and it is possible that with more precise accuracy of combination, and an offensive more resolutely sustained, they might have attained their purpose, through the mistaken primary dispositions of the British, who, though recognizing themselves to be for the time on the defensive, nevertheless, for political reasons, advanced their front of operations to a point with which, as it proved, they could not secure their communications. From the worst consequences of this error they were saved by the gallantry and skill with which advantage was taken of the defective co-operation that marked the opening of the campaign by the Boers; and there can be also little question that the wholesome respect for their fighting qualities, thus established at the beginning of hostilities, had a most beneficial effect for them, in discouraging attack by an enemy, who, though brave and active, constitutionally prefers a waiting game to an assault. Thus the ultimate fate of Ladysmith was settled in the fortnight of operations that preceded the investment.

CHAPTER II

THE OPENING CAMPAIGN IN NATAL TO THE INVESTMENT OF LADYSMITH (OCTOBER 11—NOVEMBER 2)

THE evident exposure of Natal to the first and heaviest attack of the enemy, and the necessity so to provide for its defence as to gain the time necessary for reinforcements to arrive, engaged very early the anxious attention of the Imperial and local authorities. The latter especially felt the greater solicitude, which is natural to those whose interests are immediately threatened. As early as May 25, before the Bloemfontein Conference between Sir Alfred Milner and President Kruger, the Natal Ministry notified Mr. Chamberlain that, owing to Boer preparations across the border, the scattered British in the neck of Natal were getting uneasy, and the Ministry itself nervous, at the prospect of war. These representations were repeated more urgently in the middle of June, and a month later a request was made to be confidentially informed of the proposed plan for defence. When this was communicated, it appeared that General Sir Penn Symons, commanding the Imperial troops in Natal (who afterward was the first general officer killed in the war), considered that with the force then at his disposal—something over 5,000 men of all arms—he could do no more than hold the railroad as far as Hattingh Spruit, some five miles north of Dundee, thereby protecting the collieries. To advance as far as Newcastle he estimated would require 2,000 more, while to hold Laing's Nek an addition of 5,600 would be needed.

These calculations, as is now known, fell far short of the necessities of the case, but they sufficiently alarmed the Colonial Government, and upon its remonstrance the British Cabinet, on August 3, decided to send a reinforcement of 2,000 men.

On the 6th of September the Governor of Natal telegraphed at length to London many menacing symptoms observable among the

Boers, from which war was believed to be inevitable, and urged the immediate despatch of troops sufficient to protect the colony. In response to this, orders were issued on September 8 for 5,700 men to start from India, and a small additional force from England itself, making a total of from seven to eight thousand. These were expected to arrive, and actually did for the most part arrive, between October 12 and 19, but even so were barely in time for the critical moment. They were also only sufficient imperfectly to defend the colony, and were by no means adequate to the offensive purpose which the Boer Government, in its ultimatum, professed to discern.

Meanwhile, on the 25th of September, Glencoe had been occupied by a detachment from Ladysmith, while reinforcements were sent to the latter. It had by this time been recognized that the attempt to hold the more advanced positions, such as Newcastle and Laing's Nek, would expose the forces so placed to the fate of isolation which afterward befell Ladysmith. The course of both the Imperial and colonial governments at this period was much affected by a wish not to precipitate hostile action on the part of the Boers; for, in general, war was not desired by the British, and, in particular, they were as yet unready. On the 28th, however, such definite and threatening movements were reported that the Natal Ministry decided at all hazards to call out the volunteers, although it had apprehended that this step would be considered practically equivalent to a declaration of war.

The increase of force in Natal to 15,000 men determined the sending out of an officer superior in rank to General Symons. Sir George White, designated for this duty, reached Cape Town October 3, and in view of the serious news he there received, proceeded at once to Durban. On the 9th, the day the Boer ultimatum was issued, he had at Pietermaritzburg an interview with the Governor, in which he expressed his disapproval of the position at Glencoe — an opinion in which other officers of rank present coincided. The Governor replied that General Symons had thought it safe, even before the Indian contingent arrived; that the step had been taken to assure the coal supply ; and that to recede from it now would involve grave political consequences, disheartening the loyal, and tending to encourage a rising among the blacks and the disaffected Dutch. Without changing his opinion as to the military error involved, Sir George White resolved to allow the detachment to remain. The decision thus taken finally constituted the British military situation in Natal when the campaign opened ; namely, an advanced detachment of three or four thousand at Glencoe and Dundee, a main body of eight to ten thousand at Ladysmith, with smaller posts guarding the communications in rear of the latter.

The greater exposure of Natal, owing to its nearness to the Boer States, had determined the concentration upon it of the bulk of the British forces in South Africa, including the reinforcements so far ordered ; by the arrival of which it was expected that there would by the end of October be 22,000 troops in South Africa. It was not till October 7 that was issued the first order to mobilise, summoning 25,000 of the Army Reserve to join the colours.

The necessities of Natal left but scant numbers to Cape Colony, which was comparatively of less consequence, because the points of vital importance to Great Britain lay near the sea-coast, protected by their mere remoteness from any speedy attack. On the far inland borders of the colony the situation soon reduced itself to that with which we were so long familiar. The four or five thousand men available at the outbreak of the war for the defence of the long frontier, extending over five hundred miles, from the Basutoland boundary to Mafeking, were obliged by the necessities of the case to concentrate; which they did at Mafeking and Kimberley. There they were speedily invested; and, being thus held in check, the border country, including the important railroad junctions of De Aar, Naauwport and Stormberg, lay freely open to the enemy. The seriousness of this military condition was much increased by the well-known political fact that the Dutch population of the region sympathized more or less actively with the Boers. In fact many of them, upon the opening of hostilities, crossed the border to join the forces of the Orange Free State.

On the 9th of October, 1899, the Transvaal Government presented an ultimatum. After recounting the political grievances of which it complained, it demanded that all points of mutual difference should be settled by arbitration, or other peaceful means, that the British troops near the Transvaal border should be withdrawn, that the recent reinforcements be removed altogether from South Africa, and that those still on the sea should not be landed. If a satisfactory answer were not received by 5 P.M., October 11, the action of the British Government would be regarded as a formal declaration of war. War therefore may be considered as having been formally initiated by the Transvaal, at the day and hour thus fixed.

For some time prior to the opening of hostilities, the armed men of both the South African Republic and the Free State had been assembling in force on their respective frontiers toward Natal; the latter less rapidly than the former, its military preparation not having received as full development as that of its ally, who for some years had been contemplating the possibility of war and accumulating material. The Transvaalers came in rapidly, and already by the end of September had gathered in numbers enough to warrant a speedy advance, before the expected reinforcements from India should reach the enemy.

There is good reason to believe that it was intended to issue the ultimatum on October 2, a week before its actual date; but there occurred the unpleasant surprise of finding that neither in food nor in ammunition were the supplies at hand sufficient to justify an immediate forward movement. The defect of imperfect transport organisation, inherent to hastily levied irregular troops, made itself at once felt. The delay doubtless strengthened both parties, but, as usual, inured most to the benefit of the one then on the defensive.

The first transports from India began to arrive on Tuesday, October 3, on which day also the bulk of the Natal volunteers were expected to be in their places; and in the six intervening days, preceding the ultimatum, eleven more steamers entered Durban with troops which were at once despatched to the front. General Symons took command at Dundee, Sir George White of the main body at Ladysmith.

The number of the Boers near at hand, and capable of being brought against either of the British posts, was variously estimated at the moment at from 8,000 to 13,000. There can be little doubt, however, that the latter figure was much more nearly correct; that, in fact, on October 11, the available force for the invasion rather exceeded than fell short of the higher figure. Although precise information is still lacking, there can be no doubt, from the character of the Boer operations, that rapid subsequent accessions raised their numbers in Natal to near 30,000 before the middle of November.

It is well here, on the verge of opening hostilities, to recall what has before been indicated, that the projection of the narrow neck of Natal, forming an acute salient angle between two hostile borders, gave especial facilities to the Boers to combine their movements outside the observation of the enemy, and to strike suddenly either at one of the British detachments, or at the railroad uniting them. Small bodies began to make their appearance from both quarters almost immediately after the expiry of the time set by the ultimatum, and for three or four days the ordinary reports of outpost observations and shots exchanged were continually received.

The uncertainty consequent upon these divergent demonstrations, some of which from the Free State seemed to aim at the rear of Ladysmith itself, was balanced and checked by the knowledge that the principal Transvaal force had assembled round Zandspruit, in its own territory, near the railroad, and some fifteen miles beyond Majuba Hill. There was reason also to believe that the Transvaalers would be found more enterprising and numerous than the Free State men. It was, therefore, natural to expect that the main attack would come from the north along the railroad, and from the east, where the approach from the Transvaal boundary, which is there marked by the Buffalo River, is over a country much more practicable than the western mountain range. These considerations in fact appear to have dictated the first combination of the Boers.

Within a week from the opening of hostilities, the latter had occupied Newcastle, thirty-seven miles by rail from Glencoe. On the 18th further demonstrations caused General Symons to withdraw the outpost stationed at Glencoe to the camp, which was a mile and a half west of Dundee. The following day, Thursday, he received information, which proved to be in the main accurate, that a combined movement was in progress by which his position was to be simultaneously attacked from the north and from the east. The force in the latter direction was given at 7,000—probably an excessive estimate; although, as several commandos had been reported on Wednesday to be moving from the northern toward the eastern column, it is probable that the latter was expected to make the chief attack. A British reconnaissance on the same evening had showed the enemy apparently in force some ten miles to the northward on the railway; but, if an attack from that quarter were intended, the Boer combination failed, for none was made.

General Joubert, in reporting the results, said, "Commandant Lucas Meyer (commanding the eastern force) has had an engagement with the British at Dundee. Meyer made a plan of campaign by messenger with Commandant Erasmus, who, however, did not put in an appearance." Convergent attacks, intended to be simultaneous, but starting from different quarters, are particularly liable to such mishaps.

While these two columns on the 18th were moving on Dundee, a third force of about 1,000 mounted men, under General Koch, coming from the north, passed round Glencoe to the westward, crossing the Biggarsberg, a lofty spur of nearly 6,000 feet, that extends from the western mountains almost across Natal, with occasional depressions, through one of which the railroad passes. On Thursday these took possession of Elandslaagte, a station sixteen miles north of Ladysmith, capturing one train and nearly intercepting another. Railroad communication in the rear of Symons was thus intercepted, at the moment that Meyer was advancing from the east, expecting to fall upon him in conjunction with the northern column. During the night of the 19th Meyer's force crossed the Buffalo River at Landman's Drift, ten miles east of Dundee, at 2.30 A.M. drove in the British pickets in that direction, and at daybreak was seen dotting the hill-ridges, about three miles east of the camp.

The scene of the approaching action of October 20 is the valley of a small stream, the general course of which, as nearly as can be judged from the maps, is north and south. The river-bed, or donga—to use the conveniently short South African term—is half a mile east of Dundee, the ground sloping easily toward it; while on the other side the watershed rises, slowly at first, afterward more rapidly, for a mile or more, to the ridge occupied by the Boers, which the road to Landman's crosses at a depression called Smith's Nek. The enemy were on both sides of the latter when first seen by the British. To the north of the Nek—to the Boer right—is Talana Hill, where the decisive fighting occurred, and which had to be carried by direct assault, lasting, with the intervals of cover, for nearly six hours.

The characteristics of the Hill itself, therefore, need to be understood. As described by an eye-witness, it is about eight hundred feet high from the level of the donga. The summit presents the flat table-like sky line, frequently noted in South African travel, of which Table Mountain, in Cape Town, is the conspicuous example. After a few hundred yards of gentle acclivity through open ground a wood is reached, near which is a homestead called Smith's Farm. Half way between the wood and the top is a stone wall supporting a terrace. Between the wood and this wall the ground is steep, broken and rocky. Immediately above the wall the terrace, though easy, is wide and open, and consequently exposed. The terrace crossed, the remainder of the ascent is almost perpendicular; a matter therefore of strenuous climbing under fire.

It appears from this description that the wood and the terrace afforded a certain amount of cover, as did the donga; that the first rush from the latter could be made rapidly, with, however, comparatively little shelter from a long-range fire, while to climb the wall and cross the terrace, though a short process, involved the utmost exposure. Concerning the last scene of the drama, the scaling the nearly precipitous fronts which skirted the Boers' position, the difficulty of the achievement caused the losses of the assailants there to be heaviest. It may be added that, owing to the unexpected and rapid developments of the day, most of the British fought without breakfast or other food.

As soon as the enemy were discovered a company of infantry occupied the donga, where successive reinforcements were received, and under cover of which the line prepared for the assault. At 5.30 the Boers surprised the British by opening with artillery—six guns—at an estimated distance of 5,400 yards from the British camp. To this three batteries replied, two of which were soon moved down to the town side of the donga. The artillery duel, at a range of 2,000 to 3,000 yards, continued until toward eight o'clock, when the Boers ceased firing, and General Symons gave the order to prepare for the assault. Difficult as was the task, and inferior though the assailants were in number, the conditions were such that the weak garrison of Dundee had no prospect of ultimate escape, unless they could rout the enemy with which they were engaged before the co-operating body from the north arrived.

While the action was in its early stages, at 10 A.M., scouts reported a large force approaching along the railroad. The small detachment left to guard the British camp moved out to meet and, if possible, to delay this new enemy. Besides the purely local conditions, it was essential, in the general plan of campaign, during the waiting period of inferiority, while their reinforcements were still on the sea, that the British should risk much to demoralise and daunt an enemy who, whatever their advantages otherwise, had not that military training and cohesion which facilitates rapid recovery from a reverse. Whatever the first mistake of advancing their position so far, it is impossible to withhold admiration from the rapidity and energy of the measures taken in the first fortnight of the campaign.

It was a dull, drizzling morning when the line of hungry British soldiers leaped from the donga and rushed for the wood; their batteries to the right and left sending a rapid continuous iron fire over their heads upon the hill-top, whence the Boers rained down lead upon their advance. Few dropped here; but in the wood, where for quite a while they halted, concealed rather than covered, many were struck down, and here it was that death found General Symons, who had galloped up to tell the men the hill *must* be taken. He had asked much of his men, but he spared not himself. He fell honoured and beloved; man cannot die better.

It was about 10 that Symons received his wound. Obedient to his last commands, the troops broke cover and worked their way from the wood to the wall, step by step; a few feet onward, rushed and down; again a rush and again down. Below the terrace they stopped, protected by the wall but unable to advance; for did man show head or hand, down swept the deadly fire from above. Men, however, are not of iron; eyes and hands weary; the brain and the nerves feel strain; and it is of the essence of defence that it exhausts quicker than does offence. It lacks intrinsically the moral tension that sustains; when the forward impulse is removed, the evil spirit of backwardness finds room to enter. As hours pass, this difference in moral conditions affects those which are external—saps physical endurance.

Whatever the reason, toward noon the Boer fire slackened; possibly the necessity of husbanding ammunition was felt. The British scaled the wall, crossed rapidly the terrace, and gained the foot of the last steep climb which lay between them and the enemy's position. Their artillery also moved forward, to sustain the final perilous attempt by keeping down the enemy's fire; but, despite all it could do, the loss here was great and fell especially heavily upon the officers, who exposed themselves freely. Out of seventeen of the latter that went into action with one battalion, five were killed and seven wounded; and the other regiments suffered in like manner, if not to the same degree. As the assailants got near the top, the batteries had to cease firing, unable longer to assure their aim between friend and foe. The last rush was then made with the bayonet, but, as is usual, the defendants did not await the shock of immediate contact. They broke and fled as the British advance crowned the summit, leaving there some thirty dead and wounded, besides seventy wounded in a field hospital on the reverse side of the hill. The artillery of the attack continued to move forward to Smith's Nek, whence the enemy's force was visible in full retreat. It was at 1.30 P.M. that the position, which General Yule, Symons's successor, styled "almost inaccessible," was finally carried.

The precise numbers engaged can as yet be only a matter of estimate, but there is little doubt that the assailants were inferior in number to the defenders. The former were about 2,000; the latter were by General Yule thought to be about 4,000, many of whom, doubtless, were not on the hill itself. The satisfaction of the victors, in what was certainly a splendid feat of arms, was somewhat marred by the disappearance of a body of cavalry, which at the opening of the day had been sent to work round the enemy's right — northern — flank. They had been taken prisoners, apparently by the co-operating

Boer force which had failed to come up in time for the fighting.

The following afternoon—Saturday, the 21st—a demonstration was made by this force; but it was not pushed home, being confined to a bombardment by two heavy guns—40-pounders—at a range of 6,000 yards. In prevision of such an attempt, Yule had already shifted some of his equipage, and now, finding that the hostile guns outranged his own, he removed the camp two miles to the southward, on high ground. On the 22nd, news being received of the enemy's defeat at Elandslaagte the day before, he endeavoured to cut off the fugitives at Glencoe, but the nearness of the northern Boers compelled him to desist, and finally to resume his last position. Realising from all the conditions that Dundee could not be held, unless reinforced, and that reinforcement was improbable, he decided now to retreat upon Ladysmith.

At 9 P.M. that night the British marched out, taking their transport trains, but necessarily leaving the wounded behind them. The road followed diverges from the railroad to the eastward, crossing the Biggarsberg, and coming out at a place called Beith. There it forks, the right-hand branch trending toward Ladysmith, parallel to the railroad and distant from it eight to ten miles. The march was severe, for the pace was necessarily rapid and sustained, and the roads heavy from recent rains; nor was it without serious risk from the nearness of the enemy, although the battle of Talana Hill had done much to free the eastern flank, and that of Elandslaagte the western. No molestation was experienced.

It is necessary now to narrate the operations of the Ladysmith garrison, which cannot in effect be dissociated from those of its dependant at Dundee.

The demonstrations of the Boers, in various directions, kept Sir George White in doubt as to their immediate intentions until Thursday, the 19th, when Elandslaagte was occupied by the force under General Koch. The same day word was received of the enemy's approach to Dundee. Both movements threatened to isolate the latter. On the 20th a reconnaissance toward

Elandslaagte was made by General French, who had arrived the day before from England. Thick weather prevented precise determination of the hostile numbers or position, but the general fact was established. That evening the successful results of the day's action at Dundee became known, and the next morning—Saturday, October 21—the reconnaissance was resumed under better atmospheric conditions. From a cliff between two and three miles from Elandslaagte a clear view of the enemy was obtained, and their fire drawn, which proved that both numerically and in artillery they were superior to the detachment before them. They had expected reinforcements, and those engaged in the ensuing affair were probably nearer 2,000 than to the 1,000 of two days before.

French telegraphed to Ladysmith and received a promise of more troops, the last of which arrived—the infantry by train—about 3 P.M. Meantime the enemy had quitted Elandslaagte for a ridge of rocky hills about a mile and a half south-east of the station—a position characterised as exceptionally strong by Sir George White, who witnessed the affair, but left its management in French's hands. More in detail, the ridge is described as being about 800 feet high, 800 to 1,000 yards long, and in a general sense perpendicular to the railroad; lying, therefore, south-east and north-west. At the latter extremity, nearer the road, are two marked elevations, with a neck between them, in which was the Boers' laager. Of these the westernmost is the higher, but both commanded the rest of the ridge throughout its full extent to the south-east. In front of the ridge the country, of general rolling contour, presents a shallow valley some two or three miles wide. The near side of this to the British, when the latter first advanced, was occupied by a few Boers, but these fell back quickly to their main body. In making their dispositions the Boers occupied in chief force the western elevations, intrenching their artillery on the inner and lower of the two. A thinner firing line was developed thence to the eastward, along the summit of the ridge covering the approach from the front. A flank being usually the weakest part of a line, the natural course for the assailant would be to attack in flank at the lower—eastern—extremity of the ridge, and to advance thence toward the main positions, supported in so doing by a secondary front attack by riflemen and artillery. To impede such an attempt the Boers had set up at intervals barbed wire fences. Through these, and over a broken rocky surface, the attacking column must fight its way, step by step, till the final hills were reached and could be rushed as Talana had been by their countrymen the day before.

The plan above outlined was the one adopted by General French; seven companies of infantry being allotted to the front attack, a regiment and five companies to that upon the flank. A few squadrons of cavalry accompanied the latter movement, as well to protect it when in performance as to profit by any mishap befalling the enemy. The troops formed just below and under cover of the rising ground on the hither side of the valley fronting the hostile line. The fire of the latter was drawn, and the situation of their artillery thus discovered—despite the use of smokeless powder—by the flashes of their guns, which showed the more clearly against the blackness of a big thunder cloud rising behind the Dutch positions, which enabled the British also to see distinctly the bursting of their own shrapnel over the enemy.

The usual artillery duel succeeded at a distance of 4,500 yards—two miles and a half—but from the lateness of the hour, and the amount of work ahead, no time could be lost, so the infantry operation began as quickly as possible. The front attack moved down into the valley, a firing line of three hundred men covering the space of 500 yards from end to end, its remaining companies following at intervals to support it, and to replace those who fell—to "feed" the line, keeping it at full strength.

The first part of this advance was, on account of the distance, resisted chiefly by artillery fire, which, though accurate, was seen to cause there few casualties. At 1,200 yards from the enemy's positions, being there well within rifle range, the line halted, lay down, and opened fire. The smooth surface of the ground gave little natural shelter;

what there was was found chiefly behind ant hills, of which there were very many. The musketry fire here undergone was severe, for the only diversion to it continued so far to be the British artillery, the flanking movement not having yet fully developed. Under the undivided attention of the enemy's riflemen, the line worked its way steadily forward, men dropping frequently, to within 800 yards of the summit, where they finally lay down and waited under a constant fall of shot till the bugle should summon them to the storm.

Meantime, during these last 400 yards, the flank attack was beginning. In general, the first ascent was of the rocky, broken character before noted, both here and at Talana; but, the strength of the Boer force being on the other flank, the assailants, while mounting, were covered by the slope and did not come fairly under fire until the top was reached. Then they began to fall rapidly, but a few paces further the ground dipped, and again gave momentary shelter. It was, however, but to take breath for the final rush; if rush it can be called, which meant steady, dogged bearing up against a pitiless rain of projectiles, and forcing one's way forward rock by rock, while companions drop, one by one, on either side. Six hundred yards of such work lay, before the flanking column, interrupted ever and anon by the barbed-wire obstacles, which, however, were themselves often cut down by the intensity of the fire.

Under such conditions the community of action which rests upon formal organisation and method ceases to be effectual. The momentum that endures to the end, and so effects the results of co-operation, finds its energy partly in individual character, partly in the moral fellowship of impulse and of purpose which, once imparted, remains subconscious, perhaps, but ineradicable. The man knows, or rather feels, that if he gets to the end he will find his comrades there; and that if he goes back he will not find them, but his own self-contempt. Such is unanimity, the oneness of will that comes of a common training and of common ideals, bred-in, if not inborn. So this mass of men, independent each, and yet members, each, one of the other, struggled forward, through failing light and drenching rain — for the storm had burst as the ascent began—till half the way was won. Then the bugle sounded "Charge," and the reply came cheerily up from below. The men, in the valley and on the hill, moved forward with the bayonet, still not neglecting cover, but looking now more to speed. Again, as usual, save a few of the more stubborn who were killed at their guns, the defenders did not await the shock but fled down the hills, where the cavalry that had accompanied the flank attack got among them and completed their discomfiture.

The battle at Elandslaagte was distinctly creditable to both sides, but upon the whole gave sounder cause for self-congratulation to the British than to their opponents. The former were numerically superior to the defenders, but not to an extent which countervailed even the natural advantages of the ground, further improved by measures for which time allowed.

Regarded apart from its connection with the campaign as a whole, simply as a combat unrelated to other incidents, the conception and the execution of the attack were admirable; while in the matter of military dynamic energy, to whatever source that shown on the one side or the other may be attributed, the potentiality of the attacking force was demonstrated to be greater than that of the opponent.

Still more was the action at Elandslaagte commendable, when viewed in relation to the general respective conditions of the Boers and the British in Natal at that time.

Duly to appreciate the merits and the results of these two successive days of fighting, at Talana and at Elandslaagte, it must be remembered that the British in a general sense, and at Dundee locally as well, were upon the defensive, and that the Boer movements were each a part of one general plan directed, and most properly, to overwhelm and destroy the detachments—Dundee and Ladysmith—in detail; they together being rightly considered one fraction of the enemy's whole force, present or hurrying over sea. So regarded, the vigour with which the British took the initiative, assumed the offensive, themselves in turn attacking in detail, and severely punishing, the separate factors of the enemy's combination, is worthy of great praise. Sir Penn Symons is perhaps entitled to the greater meed because to him fell, with the greater burden, the greater opportunity, to which he proved not unequal.

Such men were worthy of the steady forward gallantry shown by officers and men. Both leaders and led easily carry off the palm from the more phlegmatic opponents, who failed to sweep them away. The result was to save Ladysmith, or rather—what was most really important—to save the organized force that was there shut in. The brilliant antecedent campaign, the offensive right and left strokes, the prompt and timely resolve of Yule to retreat just as he did, and the consequent concentration, utterly frustrated the Boers' combinations, and shattered antecedently their expectations of subduing the British by the cheaper method of exhaustion. The failure was not only signal, but in the end discreditable; for while success is no sure proof of merit, nor its opposite of indesert, the wide miscalculation of the ultimate result, which kept the Boers so long inactive before Ladysmith, and saved Natal, while reinforcements were well known all the while to be hasting across the sea, is entitled to scant respect from any indications in its favour. The faulty execution of the original plan, which enabled the enemy to concentrate and to accumulate adequate means of resistance, and the subsequent underestimate of the endurance of the garrison, bear the same mark. In issuing their ultimatum, in opening the campaign, in combining against Dundee, and finally in investing Ladysmith, the Boers exceeded decisively that five minutes of delay upon which, to use Nelson's words, turns victory or defeat; and the loss of time, as yet only serious, through the procrastinations of the siege became irremediable.

It is noticeable that the returns of casualties at Elandslaagte do not perfectly bear out extreme conclusions as to the fatal preponderance of the defence over the offence in modern warfare. As reported soon after the action, the British lost in killed, 55; in wounded, 199. Of the Boers, 65 dead were found on the ground; others, estimated—guessed is perhaps more correct—at 50, were killed in pursuit by the cavalry. Their wounded is not stated, but there were many among the three hundred prisoners taken. It is true, certainly, that in this affair not only was the British attack well combined, but their superiority in numbers was considerable. Still, after all deductions, the greater loss of the defendants casts doubt, either upon their marksmanship or upon the prevalent theory that the effects of modern weapons are revolutionary. As a historical fact, a front attack upon intrenched men, even irregulars, has been a desperate business as far back, at least, as Bunker Hill and Fort Moultrie.

Twenty-four hours after Elandslaagte, at 9 P.M., Sunday, October 22, Yule's men started on their march of sixty miles, of mountain climb and over rain-drenched roads, to Ladysmith. Their own work at Talana Hill had secured the left flank of their retreat, by the demoralization of Meyer's force; to protect their right, the increasing numbers and threatening movements of the enemy west of the railroad impelled Sir George White to further action. On the 24th he moved out a strong force, which discovered the enemy at Rietfontein, seven miles from Ladysmith, on a ridge west of, and parallel to, the Glencoe road; their artillery intrenched in the centre, and supported by infantry upon commanding elevations at either end. The British drew up on a parallel ridge, to the eastward, and an action ensued, confined mainly to artillery at 3,000 yards. In the end the Boers, chiefly a body of Free State men, evacuated their positions about 2 P.M. and retired to the westward. Pursuit was not attempted. The security and junction of Yule's detachment was the prime immediate necessity, and it was by this fully apparent that the time was come when offensive returns, on the part of the greatly outnumbered British, must be limited to those needed to insure necessary delay before final inevitable interception and investment. It was no occasion for displays of military fancy sparring.

Shortly after noon of Thursday, October 26, Yule's column marched into Ladysmith—"done up," telegraphed White, "but in good spirits and only need rest." The lamented Steevens, with his graphic pen, has described for us the pride, pomp and circumstance of the return of the men who had stormed Talana Hill, and had still before them the grim protracted realities of Ladysmith.

"Before next morning was gray in came the 1st Rifles. They plashed uphill to their blue-roofed huts on the south-west side of the town. By the time the sun was up they were fed by their sister battalion, the 2nd, and had begun to unwind their putties. But what a sight! Their putties were not soaked and not caked; say, rather, that there may have been a core of puttie inside, but that the men's legs were imbedded in a serpentine cast of clay. As for their boots, you could only infer them from the huge balls of stratified mud they bore round their feet. Red mud, yellow mud, black mud, brown mud — they lifted their feet toilsomely; they were land plummets that had sucked up specimens of all the heavy, sticky soils for fifteen miles. Officers and men alike bristled stiff with a week's beard. Rents in their khaki showed white skin; from their grimed hands and heads you might have judged them half red men, half soot-black. Eyelids hung fat and heavy over hollow cheeks and pointed cheekbones. Only the eye remained—the sky-blue, steel-keen, hard, clear, unconquerable English eye — to tell that thirty-two miles without rest, four days without a square meal, six nights—for many—without a stretch of sleep, still found them soldiers at the end.

"That was the beginning of them; but they were not all in till the middle of the afternoon — which made thirty-six hours on their legs. The Irish Fusiliers tramped in at lunch-time — going a bit short some of them, nearly all a trifle stiff on the feet—but solid, square and sturdy from the knees upward. They straightened up to the cheers that met them, and stepped out on scorching feet as if they were ready to go into action again on the instant. After them came the guns — not the sleek creatures of Laffan's Plain, rough with earth and spinning mud from their wheels, but war-worn and fresh from slaughter; you might imagine their damp muzzles were dripping blood. You could count the horses' ribs; they looked as if you could break them in half before the quarters. But they, too, knew they were being cheered; they threw their ears up and flung all the weight left them into the traces.

"Through fire, water and earth, the Dundee column had come home again." *

The undeniable error of placing an advanced detachment in Dundee had thus been redeemed; at much material cost, it may be granted, but the moral gain probably exceeded, and the gallant author of the mistake paid for his error with his life. General Symons died in Dundee on the day his column came in touch with the Ladysmith force.

In the ensuing week the Boers in largely superior numbers closed rapidly down upon the now concentrated British, who on their part strained every nerve to accumulate strength and resources, and to secure time, by imposing caution and delay upon the enemy.

It was in an attempt of this kind that the disaster at Nicholson's Nek was incurred. The enemy had appeared in great numerical strength upon the hills, from three to five miles north of the town, and thence round to the eastward, over a line of seven or eight miles. A reconnaissance in force was planned

* "From Cape Town to Ladysmith," p. 79.

for Monday, October 30, and in support of it, to secure the British left flank, a detachment of a dozen companies of infantry with a mountain battery started at 11 P.M., Sunday, to march nearly due north, up the bed of a stream called Bell's Spruit, to occupy the elevation known as Nicholson's Nek. Advance along the broken, rock-strewn, and unfamiliar watercourse was necessarily slow, but was unmolested until about two hours before daybreak, when some boulders were rolled down from a neighbouring height and fell among the mules of the battery, which was in the middle of the column, preceded and followed by infantry. The terrified creatures broke from their keepers, turned, and dashed in the darkness through the rear of the division, where several shots were fired into them by the startled soldiers, unable to see the character of the rush they felt. Confusion necessarily ensued, and the panic spread to the other ammunition animals, which stampeded. Order was with difficulty restored, and the detachment, thus arrested, at daybreak found itself still two miles short of its destination. It was not thought expedient to press on; and refuge, rather than position, was sought upon a hill near by, which looked defensible, but upon climbing was found to be commanded from several quarters. These were soon occupied by the Boers, and after a resistance protracted to about 3 P.M., the detachment was compelled to surrender. Something over a thousand men were thus lost to the besieged, who could ill afford it. The missing—mostly prisoners—amounted to 843. On the field 52 were found dead, and 150 wounded were brought back to Ladysmith. Less than 100 escaped.

The rest of the British movement was successfully carried out, the enemy retiring before them; but although all the troops were out, except those absolutely needed for garrisoning the works, the enemy's field bases —"laagers"—could not be reached. Their numbers and dispositions so far made were observed; but the approaching powerlessness of the British for decisive offensive action was also shown. Upon returning to camp at 2 P.M., it was happily found that a naval brigade from the cruiser "Powerful," lying at

Durban, had reached Ladysmith with long range and heavy guns. These were quickly got into position and soon silenced a Boer 40-pounder, which at daybreak had opened fire on the town from a hill between two and three miles to the northward. A few hours later news came in of the reverse at Nicholson's Nek.

The naval guns arrived in the nick of time, the very day that the enemy got their first heavy piece at work, and but three days before all communication with outside was intercepted. The closeness of the shave emphasizes the military value of unremitting activity in doing, and unremitting energy in retarding an opponent. At one end of the line Talana Hill, Elandslaagte, Rietfontein ; at the other, 200 miles away, a naval division rushing guns ashore and to the railroad. The result, a siege artillery opportunely mounted to keep the adversary at distance.

"The enemy's guns," telegraphed Sir George White, October 30, "range further than our field guns. I have now some naval guns, which have temporarily silenced, and I hope will permanently dominate, the enemy's best guns, with which he has been bombarding the town at a distance of over 6,000 yards." "Our forces were seriously outnumbered and our guns outranged" (yesterday), wrote a correspondent in Ladysmith, "until the arrival of the naval brigade, who rendered excellent service." "The prompt assistance rendered by the Navy 190 miles inland has added immensely to the defensive strength of the position, which now depends upon keeping down the enemy's artillery fire. If the siege guns of the Boers can be controlled, the rifle fire of a stout-hearted force ought to render a successful assault impossible."

The naval guns were six—two 4.7 inch, and four long 12-pounders. They were mounted on carriages hastily extemporised for the emergency by Captain Percy Scott, of the Royal Navy, and, as they outranged the army field guns by full 2,000 yards, they extended by at least double that distance the diameter of the circle of investment imposed upon the enemy.

On the 2nd of November telegraphic

communication between Ladysmith and the outer world was broken, and the same day railroad communication was intercepted; the last train out carrying General French to take a cavalry command at Cape Town. The brief, exciting, and brilliant prelude to the war was concluded, and a great and controlling centre of national and military interest had been established by the isolation of some 13,000 British in the midst of foes whose numbers are not even yet accurately known, but of whose great superiority in that respect there can be no doubt. For a hundred and eighteen weary days the blockade lasted, until, on February 28, 1900, the advance of the relieving force entered the place.

Almost simultaneously with the beginning of the investment, on the 31st of October, General Sir Redvers Buller arrived from England at Cape Town to take chief command of the British forces in South Africa. The second period of the war now opened, before recounting which it will be necessary to summarize the general situation at date, as constituted by many preliminary occurrences in different, and even remote, quarters of the world. Up to the present, success had seemed to lie with the Boers, but the appearance was only superficial. Their plan had been well designed, but in execution it had failed; and while the failure is to be laid in part to a certain tardiness and lack of synchronism in their own movements, it was due yet more to the well-judged, energetic, and brilliantly executed movements of Sir George White and Sir Penn Symons, which utilised and completed the dislocation in the enemy's action, and so insured the time necessary for organising defence upon an adequately competent scale.

"Sir George White's force," wrote Spencer Wilkinson, on the 18th October, "is the centre of gravity of the situation. If the Boers cannot defeat it their case is hopeless; if they can crush it they may have hopes of ultimate success." * The summary was true then, and is now. In the preliminary trial of skill and strength the Boers had been worsted.

NOTE.—The effective British force shut up in Ladysmith on November 2 was 13,496, besides which there were 249

* "Lessons of the War," p. 13.

sick and wounded; total, 13,745. The Boer force in Natal is not accurately known, but is roughly reckoned at double the British; say 30,000. This estimate is probable, both from the extent of their operations, and because they ought to have had at least so many. It would be more to their discredit to have had fewer than to fail with more. The non-military element in Ladysmith raised the number of the besieged to about 21,000.

CHAPTER III

THE COLONIES AND THE TRANSPORTS

IN matters accessory to the War in South Africa, two stand conspicuous, as worthy of note by such as interest themselves in clearly comprehending those contemporary facts of which the import is not merely local, but universal. As in all theatres of war, and in all campaigns, there exist in South Africa particular conditions, permanent or transient, to utilise or to overcome which introduces into the character of the forces employed, and into their operations, specific variations, distinguishing them from methods elsewhere preferable. Such differences, however, being accidental in character, involve questions strictly of detail—of application—and do not affect the principles which are common to warfare everywhere. To the casual reader, therefore, they are less important to master and to retain in mind, however necessary to be observed, in order to apprehend the relative advantages and disadvantages of the parties to the conflict, and so to appreciate the skill or the defects shown by either in the various circumstances that arise.

In South Africa such specific differences are to be found, not only in the features of the country, which are more than usually exceptional, or in the contrast of characteristics between the two races engaged, which from the military point of view is very marked, but notably in the uncertainties and impediments attending the lines of communication by which the British army must be sustained nearly a thousand miles from the sea. These embarrassments are manifest in the great length and small capacity of the single-track railroad — 750 miles to Bloemfontein and over 1,000 to Pretoria; in the difficulty and slowness of transport by all other means; in the problems of water, and of pasturage, as affected by the wet and dry seasons; in the effect of all these upon mobility, and in the influence on questions of transport, and of all mobile services, exercised by the regional sickness that rapidly destroys the greater part of non-acclimated horses.

Communications dominate war; to protect long lines of communication from serious interference by raids demands an ample mobile force.

These are general principles of warfare, universally applicable. The questions of water, pasturage, and horse sickness are special to South Africa, as is also in some degree the inadequate railway system; and these constitute conditions which modify the local application of general principles. Two factors, however, have appeared in this war which, while they characterise it especially, are gravely significant to those who would fain seek in current events instruction for the future, whether of warning or of encouragement. These are the almost complete failure of the British Government and people to recognise at the beginning the bigness of the task before them; and, in the second place, the enthusiasm and practical unanimity with which not South Africa only but the other and distant British colonies offered their services to the mother country. The philosophical reflector can scarcely fail to be impressed with this latter political fact; for it has illustrated vividly the general truth that, when once men's minds are prepared, a simple unforeseen incident converts what has seemed an academic theory, or an idle dream, into a concrete and most pregnant fact.

The naval battle of Manila Bay will to the future appear one of the decisive events of history, for there the visions of the few, which had quickened unconsciously the conceptions of the many, materialised as suddenly as unexpectedly into an actuality that could be neither obviated nor undone. What Dewey's victory was to the over-sea expansion of the United States, what the bombardment of Fort Sumter in 1861 was to the sentiment of Union in the Northern States, that Paul Kruger's ultimatum, summarizing in itself the antecedent disintegrating course of the Afrikander Bond, was to Imperial Federation. A fruitful idea, which the unbeliever had thought to bury under scoffs, had taken root in the convictions of men, and passed as by a bound into vigorous life — perfect, if not yet mature. In these months of war, a common devotion, a common service, a common achievement, will have constituted a bond of common memories and recognised community of ideals and interests. To a political entity these are as a living spirit, which, when it exists, can well await the slow growth of formal organisation, and of compact, that are but the body, the material framework, of political life.

It is evident enough that the Transvaal War was the occasion, not the cause, of the manifested unity of purpose which resulted in immediate common action between communities so far apart, geographically, as the British Islands, Canada and Australasia. As early as July 11 the Governor of Queensland had telegraphed that in case of hostilities the colony would offer two hundred and fifty mounted infantry, and on September 29 the Governor of New Zealand sent a message of like tenor. Before the Boer ultimatum was issued, Western Australia and Tasmania had volunteered contingents. The other colonies rapidly followed these examples. There were, indeed, here and there manifestations of dissent, but they turned mainly upon questions of constitutional interpretation and propriety, and even as such received comparatively little attention in the overwhelming majority of popular sentiment.

The attitude of the Imperial Government throughout was strictly and even scrupulously correct. The action of the colonies was left to be purely voluntary, the aid accepted from them being freely proffered, and the expenses of equipment and transportation by themselves voted. Not till the landing of the colonial troops in Africa were they taken into pay as an integral part of the Imperial forces, to which they were assimilated also as regards support in the field, and in matters of pension for wounds and other compassionate allowances.

The rapidity which characterised the movements on the part of the various colonies affords the most convincing proof, not only of the cordial readiness of their co-operation, but of the antecedent attitude of thoughtful sentiment toward the home country and the interests of the Empire, which is a far more important matter than the relatively scanty numbers of men sent. Imperial Federation is a most momentous fact in the world's history, but in material results it concerns the future rather than the present.

On the 9th of October the Boer ultimatum was issued. On the 23rd the contingent from British Columbia left Vancouver, to cross the continent to Quebec, where the Canadian force was to assemble; and from that port, on the 30th of the same month, the "Sardinian," of the Canadian line, sailed with 1,049 officers and men. The New Zealanders and part of those from New South Wales had already started, and by the 5th of November there was left in Australia but one small steamer's load, of less than one hundred men with their horses, which was not already at sea speeding for Cape Town. To what was known officially as the First Colonial Contingent the Australasian colonies contributed 1,491 officers and men.

It is impossible to an American reading these facts not to recall that there was a day when troops, from what were then North American colonies, fought for Great Britain in the trenches at Havana, and before Louisburg in Cape Breton, as well as in the more celebrated campaigns on the lines of Lake Champlain and the St. Lawrence. But—and herein is the contrast between past and present that makes the latter so vitally interesting—neither mother country nor colonies had then aroused to consciousness of world-wide conditions, for which indeed the time was not yet ripe, but by which alone immediate and purely local considerations can be seen in their true proportions, and allowed proper relative weight. From those old wars the mother country expected but an addition to her colonial system, to be utilised for her own advantage; the colonists, outside the love of adventure inherent in their blood, were moved almost wholly by the jealousies and dangers of the immediate situation, as the South African colonists have in part been in the present instance. American concern naturally, inevitably as things then were, did not travel outside the range of American interests, American opportunities, American dangers, while the British Government regarded its colonies as all mother countries in those days did. Consequently, when the wills of the one and the other clashed, there was no common unifying motive, no lofty sentiment—such as that of national Union was in 1861 to those who experienced it—to assert supremacy, to induce conciliation, by subordinating immediate interest and conviction of rights to its own superior claim.

After making due allowance for mere racial sympathy, which in the present contest has had even in the neutral United States so large a share in determining individual sympathies, the claim of an English newspaper is approximately correct, that the universal action of the colonies, where volunteering far exceeded the numbers first sent, "indicates what is the opinion of bodies of free men, widely separated by social and geographical conditions, concerning the justice and necessity of the quarrel in which we are now engaged." But this takes too little account of the much more important political fact that cold opinion was quickened to hot action by the sentiment of the unity of the Empire, an ideal which under different conditions may well take to Imperial Federation the place that the Union occupied in American hearts and minds in 1861. Alike in breadth of view and in force of sentiment, nothing exceeds the power of such an ideal to lift men above narrow self-interest to the strenuous self-devotion demanded by great emergencies. Should this be so in the present case, and increase, Imperial Federation and the expansion of the United States are facts, which, whether taken singly or in correlation, are secondary in importance to nothing contemporaneous.

Nowhere was the failure of the British Government to comprehend the largeness, at once of the current struggle and of its Imperial opportunities, more evident than in the wording of its momentary rejection of the second proffered help from the self-governing colonies. To the offer of the Canadian Government on November 3, the British Ministry on the 8th replied that circumstances then were such that the necessity of a second contingent was not apparent. It may be that, to quote again a contemporary utterance, "It has been decided that the forces so contributed shall rather serve to assert a principle than to constitute a serious burden on the colonies"; and it is doubtless more judicious to accept less, and charily, of a too eager giver than to overtask his benevolence. Nevertheless, a more guarded and contingent refusal would have shown better appreciation of current conditions, and of the Imperial possibilities involved in the continued and increased participation of the colonies in an Imperial war.

In order not to revert again to the matter of colonial participation, it may be well to state here that the reverse of Methuen at Magersfontein, on December 11, occasioned a casual suggestion in the London *Times* of the 14th that "the colonies, whose forces are especially suited for the exigencies of the present struggle, have already offered in some instances to increase the strength of their contingents . . . and should now be invited to do so." Official invitation was not awaited. The colonies took the initiative by asking if reinforcements would be acceptable, and upon an affirmative reply the additional troops and sums required received the votes of men of all parties; Buller's first repulse at Colenso, and the news of Roberts' appointment to the chief command in South Africa, contributing simultaneously to harden determination and to swell enthusiasm. Whatever may be thought of the judgment of the Ministry in the first refusal, which but reflected the slowness with which both it and the nation it represented aroused to the magnitude of their task, there can be little doubt that the general outcome was favourable beyond all antecedent probability to nurturing the growth of the Imperial sentiment. In the second effort Canada sent 1,969 officers and men, Australasia 1,843. From the number of horses accompanying them it is evident that these were chiefly, if not all, mounted troops; the kind especially needed for the seat of war.

The figures given yield a grand total of 6,352 sent from the Canadian and Australasian colonies in the more formal organization. To these are to be added from New Zealand and Australia some 2,700 irregular horse, raised from among the men who live there in the open, not previously enrolled, and corresponding in general characteristics to the Rough Riders of our recent war in Cuba. India also sent a contingent of 2,437 men and officers. Up to this moment of writing, no certain account of the number of colonial troops furnished by the South African colonies has been accessible to me. Speaking in public recently, Mr. Chamberlain has said that more than 30,000 men had been offered by the self-governing colonies. Early in December it was estimated that, including the forces in Kimberley, Mafeking, and Rhodesia, Cape Colony had already 10,000 in service. In February, an official, but incomplete, and therefore a minimum, list attributed 7,158 at that time to Natal. Combining these various statements, and reckoning at 12,000 the contingents from the other self-governing colonies (excluding India), at the time of Chamberlain's speech (May 11), it seems probable that British South Africa put into the field from 20,000 to 25,000 men. This conclusion agrees substantially with one furnished to the author from an independent source, using other data.

In its entirety, the contribution of some 12,000 troops—more or less*—from the greater

* More have sailed since the above information, but exact figures are wanting to the author.

remote dependencies does not indeed loom very large alongside the truly gigantic figure of 166,277 officers and men, who, between the 20th of October and the 31st of March, were despatched for South Africa from the ports of the United Kingdom; in which number are not included those drawn from India and from England prior to the earlier date, and who constituted the bulk of the force shut up in Ladysmith under Sir George White. But the practical importance of a common sentiment—of a great moral fact—is not to be measured by figures only. The idea of Imperial Federation justifies itself to the intelligence as well as to the imagination, resting upon the solid foundation of common interests as well as of common traditions.

In the adjustment of relative importance in men's intellects—which must precede any useful adjustment of mutual relations, benefits and responsibilities, by former political agreement—the colonies on the one hand will have to recognize the immensely greater burden, as indicated by the above figures and by the size of the fleet, borne by the United Kingdom. The latter on its part must acknowledge, as in practice she has done, not merely the right of the colonies to their local administration and self-government, but also the indispensable contribution to the mutual interests of all parts in the Federation, that results from local naval bases of operations in many decisive parts of the world, resting everywhere upon the one sure foundation for such bases—an enthusiastically loyal, self-dependent, and military population. Military power, in analysis, consists principally of two factors—force and position—and if the greater wealth and population of the home country causes it to exceed in the former, the dispersion and character of the dependencies contribute decisively to the latter.

The transportation of the above immense body of soldiers, with all the equipment and supplies of war needed for a protracted campaign a distance of 6,000 miles * by sea, is an incident unprecedented, and in its success unsurpassed, in military history. The nature of the war, it is true, removed from the undertaking

* The distance from Southampton, the chief though not the only port of departure, to Cape Town is 5,978 miles.

all military or naval risk ; there was in it nothing corresponding to the anxious solicitude imposed upon the British generals, by the length of their thin railroad line and its exposure in numerous critical points to a mobile enemy. But as a triumph of organisation—of method, of system, and of sedulous competent attention to details—the performance has reflected the utmost credit not only upon the Admiralty, to which, contrary to the rule of the United States, this matter is intrusted, and which is ultimately responsible both for the general system in force and for the results, but also upon the Director of Transports, Rear-Admiral Bouverie Clark, to whose tenure of this office has fallen the weighty care of immediate supervision. To success in so great an undertaking are needed both a good antecedent system and a good administrator; for administration under such exceptional conditions, precipitated also at the end by the rapid development of events, means not merely the steady running of a well-adjusted and well-oiled machine, but continual adaptation—flexibility and readiness as well as precision, the spirit as well as the letter. When a particular process has had so large a share in the general conduct of a war, a broad account of its greater details is indispensable to a complete history of the operations.

The number and varied distribution, in place and in climate, of the colonial or foreign posts occupied by the British army at the present time, and the extensive character of its operations abroad, during war and peace, for two centuries have occasioned a gradual elaboration of regulation in the transport system, to which, by the necessity of frequent changes of troops, are added an extent and a continuity of practical experience that has no parallel in other nations. These have vastly facilitated the unprecedented development demanded by the present war. A leaven of experimental familiarity, by previous personal contact with the various problems to be solved, suffices to permeate the very large lump of crude helplessness that may be unavoidably thrown upon the hands of regimental officers; and even where such personal experience has been wholly wanting to a particular ship's company, the minuteness of the regulations, if intelligently followed, gives a direction and precision to action, which will quickly result in the order and convenience essential to the crowded life afloat. Nowhere more than on board ship does man live ever face to face with the necessity of order and system, for there always the most has to be disposed in the least space.

When a ship is engaged for the government service wholly—but not otherwise—she is known officially as a "transport"; when passage for troops is taken, but the ship is not entirely at the government's disposal, she is a "troop freight ship." In the former capacity, to adapt her to her new employment, she passes under the charge of designated naval officers for particular fitting; the time for which, in this war's practice, has not exceeded two weeks for infantry or four for cavalry transports. Upon preparation completed ensues an immediate inspection by a mixed board of army, navy, and medical officers before the ship proceeds to the place for embarkation. The aim necessarily is to keep this process well in advance of the mobilisation of the troops, and incites to beneficial rivalry the

War Office and the Admiralty, between which there must be full mutual understanding and prevision, as to the readiness of the transports, the ports of assembly, the numbers and quantities of men, of horses, and of material of all kinds, to be carried in each vessel.

When an embarkation is to take place, the position and arrangement of the ships at the docks, the number and regiments of men assigned to each are arranged, have been arranged, often many days before. The system and manner are laid down by regulation, from the time the detachment leaves the post where it has been stationed until the ship is ready to cast off from the dock and go to sea. Each man takes with him in the car, from the starting point, his sea kit and immediate personal equipment, from which he is not permitted to part until it is handed aboard for stowage in the precise place assigned to it in the vessel. The muskets, when carried by the men on the journey, are marked each with a label corresponding to the rack where it is to stand in the ship. Upon arrival at the port, and during the operation of transferring, a naval officer is in charge so far as general direction on the dock and on board the ship is concerned, but without superseding the military ordering and management of the troops by their own officers. The same general arrangement continues at sea. That is, the discipline, routine, and supervision of the troops are in the hands of the military officers, as though in a garrison; but they can give no orders as to the management or movements of the ship to the sea captain who commands her. On board, the mode of life is fixed by regulation—subject, of course, to the changes and interruptions inseparable from sea conditions. The hours for rising, for meals, for drills, for bed, and all the usual incidents of the common day are strictly prescribed.

With such forethought and method, ripened by long experience, results were obtained differing greatly from the headless scene of confusion attending the embarkation of our troops at Tampa, as described by witnesses. Only experience can fully meet the difficulties of a great operation of this character, and we were without experience; nor can experience like that of British officials ever be expected among us, for neither we nor any other nation has or will have the colonial responsibilities of Great Britain. The large number of seasoned sergeants and corporals, who had embarked and disembarked half a dozen times before, contributed immeasurably to the order and rapidity of the process in each shipload that went to make up the 166,000 that left England for South Africa. But while so much falls naturally to the military element, and can best be discharged by them, because by their own self-helpfulness alone it can be carried out, the choice and equipment of ships, the entire preparation and internal arrangement of them as well as the direction of their movements, coaling, etc., belong most fitly to the Navy, for the simple reason that equipment and supervision of this character are merely a special phase of the general question of naval administration and management; and no specialty—in whatsoever profession — is so successfully practised as by a man who has a broad underlying knowledge of, and wide acquaintance with, the profession in its general aspect. To this unimpeachable generalization the settled practice of the nation, whose experience in this matter transcends that of all others combined, gives incontrovertible support.

A brief detail of the methods of the first departure, October 20, 1899, will facilitate comprehension and serve for all others. That day four transports lay at Southampton Docks, to take on board Major-General Hildyard, with the first brigade of the first division of the army to be commanded by Sir Redvers Buller. The trains ran down to the wharf near the ships, the troops remaining in them until the usual officers, alighting, had placed the markers to indicate the positions for each company. At the signal the companies fell in; the regiments in quarter column. The companies then advanced successively, forming in line abreast their ship, between two gangways—one forward and one aft—along each of which was stretched a chain of men, who thus sent on board, one set the rifles, the other the sea kits and valises, which, passing from hand to hand, reached certainly and without confusion the spot where their owner knew to seek them. The company then moved off, clearing the ground for its successor, and was next divided into messes; which done, each mess, under charge of its own non-commissioned officer, went on board by a third gangway, to the living or "troop" deck. This unceasing graduated progress completed its results for the first ship by 2 P.M., when she cast off her lines and steamed out. The three others were then nearly ready, but were delayed a short space to receive a visit and inspection from the Commander-in-Chief of the Army, with a number of the distinguished higher staff-officers. Thus five thousand troops, who had slept inland the previous night, were before dark at sea on their way to South Africa.

The same scene was repeated on the Saturday, Sunday and Monday following. By the latter evening—October 23—21,672 men had sailed, the order for mobilisation having been issued just a fortnight before. Of this number more than half were of the Army Reserve; men, that is, who had served their time, gone into civil life, and now rejoined the colours.

The specific methods are sufficiently illustrated by the above, but it may be interesting to note the numbers sent in each succeeding month, for they show, on the one hand, the continuousness and magnitude of the operation, viewed as a whole, and also, incidentally, the December return indicates the slackening of the current, due to the unwarranted confidence of the people and of the government in the sufficiency of their preparations, and their underestimate of the difficulties before them. We in the United States during the Civil War more than once made a like mistake, discontinuing enlistments and discouraging volunteering.

In October, from the various ports of the United Kingdom, were despatched 28,763 officers and men; in November, 29,174; in December, 19,763; in January, 27,854. In the short month of February the spur of the December disasters began to show its results, for then the figures rose to 33,591; in March, with which month my information ends, 27,348 went out. The grand total, 166,277, may in its effects be summarized by saying that from October 20 to March 31, 162 days, an average of over one thousand men sailed daily from Great Britain or Ireland for the seat of war.

Some illustrations of the capacity of great ocean steamers for such service may also be interesting. Thus the "Cymric" carried a brigade division of artillery, 18 guns, 36 wagons, 351 officers and men, 430 horses, with all the ammunition and impedimenta, besides a battalion of infantry; in all nearly 1,600 men. Another, the "Kildonan Castle," took on an average 2,700 officers and men, on each of three voyages. The greatest number in any one trip was by the "Bavarian" —2,893.

In effect, although embarkation was not wholly confined to the great shipping ports, the vast majority of the vessels sailed from Southampton, the Thames, and the Mersey. At each of these was stationed a captain on the active list of the Navy, representing the Director of Transports at the Admiralty, and having under him a numerous staff of sea officers, engineers and clerks, by whom the work of equipment, inspecting, and despatching was supervised. After sailing, the vigilant eye of the Transport Department still followed them by further provision of local officials at foreign and colonial ports, and by the network of submarine telegraphs which has so singularly modified and centralised the operations of modern war. At Las Palmas in the Canary Islands, and at St. Vincent in the Cape de Verde, the intermediate coaling ports, a ship of war was kept always after October, the captains of which watched over the transports, cabling arrivals and departures, deciding questions of coal requirement, repairs, delays, and generally, no doubt, discharging the function noted by the midshipman, who explained that he must be going because he saw the first lieutenant's glass was turned his way.

At Cape Town, Port Elizabeth, and Durban were other local representatives—naval captains with staffs similar to those of the home ports—so that, to use a phrase of the Director of Transports, the ships were "well shepherded." It was, in fact, much the position of a man who with ten fingers manipulates the several keys of a piano. If the end crowns the work it may be said, although the end is not quite yet, that the work of transportation has been crowned. No loss of human life by preventable cause has occurred, nor has complaint been heard of serious hitch of any kind. The numbers speak for themselves.

The carriage of animals necessary for an army of the numbers transported would in any case be a weighty and troublesome task, but it has been rendered doubly so by the scanty resources of the scenes of war, by the terrible horse-sickness, and by the length of the voyage, which enfeebles the animals in a proportion ever increasing with the passage of the days. The evil becomes yet greater from the pressing needs at the front, and the importunate urgency to hasten the animals forward, over a railroad journey of hundreds of miles, without first giving them time to regain the fulness of their strength.

The importance and embarrassing nature of this factor in the campaign are hard to overestimate. The insufficient number of horses and their debility have doubtless accounted for much of the delay and seeming languor of action, which has appeared otherwise inexplicable; the utter weakness of the poor beasts having indeed been expressly alleged as the reason for failure of cavalry or of artillery in more than one critical moment. That the supply forwarded has been large, if nevertheless falling short of the demand, is shown by the transport figures, according to which, in round numbers, 50,000 horses and 39,000 mules had been shipped by the end of March. Half of the former, and the greater part of the latter, were drawn from North and South America, from Australia, and from the Mediterranean. To these figures is to be added another, yet uncertain because future, but which, when ascertained, will probably double the number of horses and mules actually used in the war, raising it, including those obtained in South Africa itself, to nearly 200,000. The monthly waste has been roughly reckoned at 5,000.

The size and multiplicity of these various operations enforce the homely, but always to be remembered, maxim that "War is business," and that in all its aspects; business in which, like every other, the aim must be the best results with the least expenditure—of money, of labour, and of life. An intermediate difficulty in the problem of getting men, horses, and supplies from England to the front of operations, and one which probably would not antecedently occur to a person inexperienced in such transactions, was the inadequate facilities at Cape Town itself, as well as of the railroads, for handling the mass of freight, animate and inanimate, unexpectedly thrust upon them. A third-class port cannot be suddenly raised to the business of one of the first class, and be found either competent or convenient. Consequently, the congestion at the docks, wharves, and railroads was very great. Many ships were kept waiting two months, or even more, for discharge; a fact which means not merely expense, though that is bad enough, but delay in operations, which in turn may be the loss of opportunity—and the equivalent of this again is prolongation of war, loss of life, and other miseries.

The practical lesson of this embarrassment at Cape Town should not be lost to those who assume too lightly that the traffic of the Suez Canal can in time of war be turned to the Cape route. The question of necessity for coaling at Cape Town, and the facilities for it should at least be exhaustively studied before accepting this solution as final, or even probable. It is evident that, for the operations of this war, the use of Port Elizabeth, Port Alfred, and East London, although they have no docks at which steamers can lie and discharge, would to some extent relieve Cape Town ; but that such relief should be effective at the front, it was necessary also that the railroads from them should be securely held up to their junctions with the main line. This was not the case at first.

It may be added, for the benefit of American readers, that this question of local congestion, and of consequent dislocation and delay of traffic and of transport, is worthy of consideration by those among us who may think that the interruption of our coasting trade, or the blockade of one or two principal harbours, can be met by transferring the business, of the former to the railroads, of the latter to other ports not blockaded. This is not so, because the local conveniences and methods, which have developed under the sifting tests of experience and actual use, cannot be transferred at short notice ; and until such transfer has been made, distribution cannot proceed. The body economic and commercial will be in the state of the body physical whose liver is congested, whose blood therefore circulates poorly, with consequent imperfect nutrition and general disorder of the system ; much where little ought to be, and little where much.

CHAPTER IV

THE WESTERN FRONTIER TO MAGERSFONTEIN AND STORMBERG—OPERATIONS OF GENERAL FRENCH ABOUT COLESBERG

AS was the case a century ago, on the eve of the French Revolution, Great Britain last year indulged too long her dream of peace, and awaked from it too late for timely preparation. Like a man who starts behindhand with his day, the catching up meant double worry, if not double work. Hildyard's brigade, which sailed October 20, had, thirty days before, been preceded by two hospital ships, three batteries of field artillery and a thousand infantry; * the last-named getting away on the 19th, only one day before Hildyard. No British field troops had then reached South Africa, save a couple

* There may have been one or two more battalions of infantry, but I have not been able to trace such.

of battalions additional to Cape Colony, and the reinforcements to Sir George White drawn mainly from India, which, with most of his corps in Natal, and despite his well-directed energy, the Boers by their superior numbers were able to round up and corral in Ladysmith in three weeks after their ultimatum was issued. There were then also on the way some fifteen hundred of the Army Service Corps, an organised body of men trained for the supply and transport service of the army, and of skilled mechanics, whose duties are to construct and maintain works of various kinds for the facilitation of army supply—transport and depot. These had sailed in the early days of October.

Such was the mighty enginery antecedently set in motion, to crush the liberties of the Transvaal. An interesting further illustration of the way decision was precipitated toward the end is found in the fact that Sir George White was gazetted Governor of Gibraltar in the last week in August, and on September 15 sailed to command the forces in Natal.

"My small experience," wrote Steevens about October 12 from the well-advanced station of Stormberg Junction, in Cape Colony, "has been confined to wars you could put your fingers on; for this war I have been looking long enough and have not found it. . . We are heavily outnumbered, and have adopted no heroic plan of abandoning the indefensible. We have an irregular force of mounted infantry at Mafeking, a regiment (regulars) at Kimberley, a regiment and a half at De Aar" (the most important of junctions), "half of the Berkshires at Naauwport, the other half here." Stormberg and Naauwport were also junctions, secondary only, if secondary, to De Aar, in the strategic importance that always attaches to crossroads. "The famous fighting Northumberlands came crawling up behind our train, and may now be at Naauwport or De Aar. Total, say, 4,100 infantry, of whom 600 mounted; no cavalry, no field guns. The Boer force available against these isolated positions might be very reasonably put at 12,000 mounted infantry, with perhaps a score of guns . . . It is dangerous—and yet nobody cares. There is nothing to do but wait—for the Army Corps that has not yet left England. Tiny forces, half a battalion in front, and no support behind —nothing but long lines of railway with ungarrisoned posts hundreds of miles at the far end of them. It is very dangerous. No supports at this moment nearer than England." *

In this brief and pregnant summary the reader will note outlined the elements characteristic of all strategic situations: the bases, the seaports; the communications, the railway lines; the front of operations, the frontier of the Orange Free State, or rather, perhaps, in this defensive—or defenceless—stage, the railroad line parallel to it, which joins De Aar, Naauwport and Stormberg.

Dangerous, sure enough; how much so needs only a glance at the map to show. Before reinforcements could arrive Sir George White was shut up in Ladysmith by forces double his own. These he held there, it is true; and the fatal delay of the Boers before his lines, reflected in their no less fatal inactivity on the frontier of the Cape Colony, whence Steevens wrote the words quoted, doubtless threw away the game; but we are now speaking, as he was then writing, of the

* "From Cape Town to Ladysmith," pp. 16–20.

time when the cards had only been dealt and the hand was yet to play. Put your marks on each of the places named—Mafeking, Kimberley, De Aar, Naauwport, Stormberg —note their individual and relative importance, the distances severing them from one another, the small bodies of men scattered among them, incapable through weakness and remoteness of supporting each other, and with no common supports behind. Mafeking is from Kimberley 223 miles; Kimberley from De Aar, 146; De Aar from Naauwport, 69; Naauwport from Stormberg 80, as the crow flies over a difficult country, at least 130 by rail. All three junctions with their intervening lines of rail, bridges, culverts and all, are little over fifty miles from the Orange River, which hereabout forms the boundary separating Cape Colony from the Free State. And White is about to be invested in Ladysmith, and the Army Corps has not yet left England.

The average length of a transport's voyage from the United Kingdom to Cape Town, as determined from 162 records, was $22\frac{1}{6}$ days. The first, with Hildyard's brigade, accomplished it in 20 days, arriving November 9; the last of the four took 25 days, coming in on the 14th. With them, and their one predecessor, 6,000 additional troops were at the latter date—five weeks after the Boers' ultimatum became operative—landed at the far base of operations, yet 500 miles by railroad from the front. Kimberley and Mafeking were then already invested, and the bombardment at both places begun. The British troops had evacuated Stormberg Junction November 3, falling back to the southward toward Sterkstrom and Queenstown; thus abandoning railroad communication between East London, one of the sea bases, and the western theatre of war toward Naauwport and De Aar. Naauwport had also been quitted at about the same time, but the Boer grasp in that central quarter was never as firm as it was to the eastward and westward. General French was early established with his cavalry at Hanover Road, midway on the line from Naauwport to De Aar, and his activity, skilfully directed against the flanks of the enemy, imparted to the latter a nervousness which the frontal attacks on the eastern line failed to produce. Naauwport was reoccupied by the British November 19, and De Aar was never by them abandoned; but the Boers on the 25th of November blew up a bridge on the line from Naauwport *via* Middelburg and Rosmead to Port Elizabeth, thereby momentarily cutting out the line from this sea base also, as their advance upon Stormberg had eliminated East London. They made also strenuous efforts, at many points, to destroy the main road from Kimberley south to Orange River, blowing up culverts and bridges, but the damage effected was afterward found to be less than had been expected, owing to the clumsiness of their methods; a fact which probably indicates that their cause was supported mainly by a rural population, and that few mechanics—townsfolk—were in their ranks.

There seems to have been no serious attempt to interrupt communications south of the Orange River, important though it was to do so. The British Corps, to the command of which Lord Methuen was assigned, assembled at the Orange River Bridge without opposition or difficulty, its concentration being effected on the 19th of November. The advance thence, in fact, began on the 21st, and on the 23rd was fought its first battle, that of Belmont.

It will be well here to summarize, map in hand, the character and result of the Boers' operations in this western theatre, during the priceless five weeks of opportunity secured to them by the over-confidence, or the remissness, or the forbearance, of their powerful enemy. The conditions differed from those in the eastern scene of war — in Natal — because there the just anxiety of the inhabitants, reflected in that of the colonial and Imperial governments, had occasioned the concentration of by far the greatest mass of available British troops.

The exposure of Natal in its more vital and strictly British interests greatly exceeded that of Cape Colony, where, owing to the remoteness of the seaboard, near which the British chiefly congregated, the first of the Boer invasion would fall upon a population strongly sympathetic with the cause of the enemy, though British in allegiance. Therefore while this disloyalty was ominous and detrimental to the British cause as a whole, direct injury to British interests was less immediately threatened. The Cape frontier, accordingly, was left defenceless, as has been shown; and in a strictly military point of view it was quite correct thus wholly to neglect one, rather than weakly to divide between two.

The consequence was that in Natal occurred during ten days the severe and nearly continuous fighting already narrated, with the result of shutting up in Ladysmith, on the direct line of any further advance contemplated by the Boers, a very strong British force; incapable, doubtless, of taking the field against the vastly superior numbers confronting it, but most capable, by numbers and position, of embarrassing any onward movement of the enemy. This aspect of the case has been too much neglected in the general apprehension.

The British in Ladysmith were doubtless an isolated and endangered garrison, the relief of which constrained the movements of its friends away from more proper objectives; but in the early days of the siege, while in the prime of the physical strength afterward drained away by hunger, and up to the time that reinforcements had arrived to bar in front the progress of the enemy, it was also to the latter what Mantua in 1796 was to Bonaparte, and Genoa in 1800 was to the Austrians prior to Marengo—a force which, if advance were attempted, would be on the rear of the army, flanking the communications. To secure these it would be necessary, before forward movement, either to carry the place by assault, suitably prepared and executed, thus sweeping it out of the way for good, or else to keep before it a detachment of sufficient strength to check any effort seriously to interrupt the communications. But this would be to divide the Boer forces, to which doubtless Joubert did not feel his numbers adequate. This was the important—the decisive—part played by Ladysmith in the campaign.

Had the Boers' "exclusiveness of purpose"—to use Napoleon's happy phrase—answered to the demands of their military situation, they would have done for military reasons what their opponents were compelled to do through unpreparedness and considerations of civil policy. They would have neglected the frontiers of Cape Colony, and concentrated their effort against the organised force which exceptionally favourable circumstances, that could not be expected either to continue or to recur, had enabled them to isolate in Natal.

What effect the failure to do this produced in the latter colony will be examined later. We have now to consider how the Boers, having decided to follow two widely divergent plans of operations, utilised the opportunity afforded them by the long period of weakness undergone by their antagonists in the debatable ground, where the frontiers of Cape Colony and the Orange Free State adjoin, along the banks of the Orange River from Basutoland to Kimberley. Remote and detached Mafeking, the news of whose deliverance comes as these lines are writing, remains a romantic episode, a dramatic centre of interest, from the heroic endurance and brilliant gallantry displayed by its garrison; but, from the practical side, the action of friend and foe, the fact of occupation and the conduct of the siege, present a military riddle not readily solved.

Noting the natural military line of the Orange River, the importance of which in more military countries would be emphasized by corresponding works of precaution, for defence and for movement, in its vicinity, it will be observed that parallel to it, at a distance of about fifty miles, within the borders of the colony, there is the stretch of railway from Stormberg, *via* Rosmead Junction and Naauwport, to De Aar. Beyond the last-named point the line, now become the main road, converges steadily and rapidly upon the border of the Free State, within a dozen miles of which it continues from the point where it crosses the Orange River until abreast the boundary between the Free State and the Transvaal. Between Stormberg and De Aar this line consists simply of the branches that there tie together the main roads, through which the principal seaports—Cape Town, Port Elizabeth, and East London—seek access to the interior. The direction, alike of the main and branch roads, as well as the position of the junctions, are doubtless determined by local considerations of topography and traffic.

Although constructed for commercial purposes, the line of rail from Stormberg to De Aar has particular military value as an advanced base of operations, from which to start, and upon which, for the initial stages, to rest a campaign. It is central as regards the extremities of the hostile frontier opposed to it ; it is moderate in length ; and, from the rapidity of transfer from end to end afforded by the railroad, it permits movements on one flank or the other to be combined with comparative facility. Add to this the convergence upon it of the several lines of supply from Cape Town, Port Elizabeth and East London, and it is evident that the line would present particular advantages for the assembling of a British army intending to invade the Free State by the most probable, because most advantageous, route, the direct highroad to Bloemfontein. It is, indeed, the key, the central military position of this theatre of war ; not geometrically, by mere measurement of distance, but as the place where converge and unite all the great communications from the opposing bases of operations, which at the first would be, for the Free State, the Orange River, and for Great Britain, the line of seaports.

The distance from the frontier and the interposition of the mountain range in the Steynsburg district would combine to make observation of preliminary movements difficult to the enemy, except, indeed, by information from the disaffected inhabitants who abounded. The secure and undisturbed tenure of this line would therefore much facilitate the British campaign, should it develop against the Free State; consequently the first aim of the Boer commanders should have been to hold, or if not able to hold, to destroy it effectually as regards steam communication.

It is as yet impossible to say exactly what was the force of the Boers on their western frontiers between the middle and the end of October. Steevens, as above quoted, thought 12,000 at the earlier date. A more likely reckoning seems to me to be 8,000, but it probably rose near the higher figure before November, and must much have exceeded it by the 1st of December, unless

British estimates are more wide of the mark than is probable. The lowest maximum for the forces of the two republics that I have seen was given by one of the Boer envoys now* in the United States; viz., 38,000. Allowing 30,000 to Natal by November 1, there is nothing immoderate in the supposition that there were then from 10,000 to 12,000 on the line of the Orange River, and from thence round to Mafeking. Personally, I believe that the totals were larger, for very considerable numbers of the Dutch population in Cape Colony and Natal joined the Boers, and the indications are that all the available men were put—and very properly—at once in the field. The emergency was great, time was invaluable, and the maintaining of a reserve, judicious in many cases, would under the conditions of the Boers have been a mere dividing and frittering of forces, by the immediate employment of which alone might success be snatched.

To allow Great Britain time to arouse, to assemble and put forth her strength, before some really decisive advantage, material or

* May 19, 1900.

moral, was gained over her, was to ensure defeat. This, however, was what the Boers did. Although they put in force successfully a *levée en masse*, and thus in point of time concentrated into action their whole fighting population, they did not with equal exclusiveness of purpose concentrate in force upon a single military objective; nor was such choice as they made dictated by sound military principle, or carried out with sound military judgment.

It so happened that the conditions at the opening of the campaign bore a curious resemblance, though on a considerably larger scale, to those attending the hostilities of 1881 in South Africa. Then, as now, the British were in number far inferior. Then, as now, they were scattered here and there in small detachments. Then the Boers had achieved successes which doubtless surprised themselves as well as their enemies, and had produced for them the unfortunate result of overvaluing their own prowess, and of inducing a secure belief that both they and their opponents, after twenty years, remained in native and acquired qualities in the same relative positions of individual superiority and inferiority that they had somewhat prematurely assumed.

It was a natural result of such prepossessions that, instead of concentrating to hold in mass some decisive position by which to prolong the war, or to destroy or capture some important detachment—such as that at Ladysmith—they should settle themselves down to sieges, to a war of posts. In 1881, of several posts they had in the same manner leisurely invested, one surrendered. They probably believed that the others would have done so, had not the British Government of that day yielded and made peace. Whatever the reasoning, it was to the method of 1881 that the Boers resorted. After the preliminary battles in Natal, already narrated, in each of which the British attacked, they settled down with facile indolence to an investment of Ladysmith.

The dissemination of the enemy on the Free State frontier, so graphically summarized by Steevens, could not induce them to crush, with the concentrated force permitted by their imposing superiority of numbers, any one of the small detachments thus fatally exposed. The place, not the force within, had military value in their eyes. To the general result contributed no doubt the tendency of local interest to dominate general considerations in a rural and loosely organised population. It was noted at the time that the principle of local operation decided not only that the Transvaal should operate chiefly in Natal, and the Orange Free State toward Cape Colony, but also determined the course of action within each state. "There has been very little moving about of burghers from one part of the Transvaal or Free State to the other. . . . In the latter, the eastern commandos have gone to Natal, the western ones to Kimberley, and to the southern ones, numbering probably less than 4,000 men altogether, have been left the double task of invading Cape Colony and keeping off the Basutos; and as the ordinary Free State burgher is much more anxious about his own farm than about turning our colony upside down, the result is that practically nothing has been done to attack the most vulnerable point in our defence."

The same correspondent, writing from Cape Town, October 25, said that there were not 3,000 men of regular troops, and no artillery, in Cape Colony when the war broke out. His means of information were doubtless better than those of Steevens, who was in Cape Town less than forty-eight hours and made his guess — 4,100 — before he had time for personal observation over the ground.

It is scarcely necessary to point out what an opportunity was here presented for a rapid succession of blows at isolated detachments, such as military history has often before witnessed. It is difficult to believe that the frontier could not have been swept clean from end to end, and the entire railroad system, essential to the advance and centralised action of the British forces, hopelessly dislocated and smashed by an operation embodying the most elementary conceptions of concentration. Instead of that the centre of the line was kept almost undisturbed, the principal demonstrations of the Boers across the border being on the flanks—Kimberley and Mafeking on their right, Stormberg and the districts north and east of it on their left; the railroad from Naauwport to De Aar, and thence to the Orange River, being scarcely molested, and for working purposes remaining intact. So far as military purpose can be inferred from military action, the effort of the Boers was concentrated — or rather localised — upon the occupation of unprotected and friendly districts in the east, where they took up scattered defensive positions, while for offensive operations they satisfied themselves with the investment of Kimberley and Mafeking.

An American correspondent—evidently not unfriendly—writing of Pretoria about October 20, records an instructive anecdote, which reveals much of the Boer idea and purpose, and suggests food for thought as to underlying causes, not unprecedented in history, which from the first, if then known, would have foretold sure defeat. "A large door on the opposite side of the room opened, and a clerk informed the Secretary (Mr. Reitz) that he was wanted in the Executive Council room. While he was collecting a number of papers on his desk I could hear the conversation of men in the adjoining room. Suddenly there was a deep roar—almost like that of a lion—and at the same time a bang on the table that made the windows rattle. And the voice—it was that of a man—continued its deep bellowing, and again there was a thundering bang on the table. 'The old President has met with some obstacle in his plans,' said the Secretary of State, smiling at my look of surprise at the sound of such a human voice, and he disappeared with an armload of papers. . . . When he returned he was chuckling to himself. 'General Cronje wants to assault Mafeking,' he said. 'He has wired that he can take the town in a hand-to-hand fight, but the old President won't listen to it. He says the place is not worth the lives of fifty burghers, and has just issued an order that Cronje is to continue the siege and simply see to it that Colonel Baden-Powell and his troops do not escape. The Council was divided; some thought that Cronje should be permitted to storm the place. The President has just ordered that one of the big siege-guns shall be sent to Cronje.' "*

* *Harper's Monthly Magazine*, May, 1900, p. 827.

Time apparently was of no account. The burghers and the Boers had only to wait open-mouthed for plums to drop—at Mafeking, at Kimberley, at Ladysmith. Mafeking very possibly was not in itself worth the lives of fifty burghers; but it was worth a great deal more if it was to be the means of detaining them before its little worth to their exclusion from action concentrated elsewhere, which their numbers would have gone to make overpowering, and which by proper direction would have been decisive—not perhaps of ultimate issues—but of those prolonged delays in which lies the best hope of a defence. It is an interesting commentary on Kruger's decision that, at the moment these lines are writing, the deliverance of Mafeking is known to have been preceded immediately by a fruitless assault of the burghers, which cost more than that presumed for the attack at the outset, which a competent general on the spot believed then would be successful. Control at a distant capital, exercised by an obstinate, overbearing old man, who, though unquestionably shrewd and acute, was equally unquestionably narrow with the narrowness of contracted experience and limited military knowledge, boded ill for the Boer cause. While Cronje at Mafeking, and Wessels at Kimberley, and Joubert at Ladysmith were waiting for a moment that never came, time was flying, the hostile reinforcements were speeding forward 300 miles a day, and the very danger of the three places was goading the British people into wide-awake activity.

Yet more imminent was the nearer opportunity, fast disappearing into the nearer danger, ultimately to become the established and fatal centre of ruin—at De Aar. "This was not the sort of fighting-ground the Boer is wont to choose," wrote one there present, "but we felt that he must come because we menaced his frontier sixty miles away, and tempted him with such an amount of stores, guns, and ammunition as would enable him to prolong his warfare at least two months longer than his own resources would permit." A somewhat narrow view this, leaving out of the account De Aar's intrinsic advantage in position; but to continue—"Every day that the Boers delayed our camp grew stronger, though this was not the case before

General Buller arrived at the Cape (October 31). Until then we had only one battalion —about 800 men—to protect stores estimated at half a million pounds; but within forty-eight hours a battery and a half—nine guns —had arrived from England, to be followed by another half battery from the Orange River." *

The position of De Aar indicated it absolutely as a point which the British must hold, fortify, and use as a depôt and base. Camps and buildings began to be laid out and put up about October 25, and stores to accumulate; ten days later came the batteries and also reinforcements; but these—400 in number — imperatively demanded by the superior importance and exposure of De Aar, which required concentration upon it, were obtained by evacuating Colesberg and Naauwport, the latter a most regrettable necessity. But what were the Boers doing while these fragments were drawing together into a single body, while batteries were arriving, and works, not yet existent, were being thrown up? They were besieging Kimberley and Mafe-

* Ralph's "Toward Pretoria," p. 97.

king, 150 and 300 miles away, and pottering about just within Cape Colony, occupying undefended towns and making proclamations of annexation. "Fancy," says the writer just quoted,—"fancy the Orange River sixty miles away, with 2,500 men (British) holding the (railroad) bridge over it, and a battalion of 1,000 men broken into five bodies of troops isolated at as many points—all, excepting the force at Orange River, inviting certain destruction." *

The concentration ordered by Buller, just mentioned, drew the British, on the left flank of their line in Cape Colony, into two principal bodies—2,500 at Orange River Station, where the railroad to Kimberley crosses the river, and some 1,500 at De Aar. Stormberg Junction on the right of the line was evacuated at the same time as Naauwport, the troops falling back upon Queenstown, fifty miles distant by rail. This abandonment of the two junctions severed from each other the right and left flanks of the general front, which extended from Stormberg to De Aar, depriving them of mutual support; a condition of

* Ralph's "Toward Pretoria," p. 104.

disadvantage that was not wholly removed until after the occupation of Bloemfontein. This gain to the Boers, however, was due to no well-combined active operations on their side, but to the mere fact that their opponents were everywhere so hopelessly weaker in numbers that it was insanity any longer to risk these small detachments in places where they ought to have been captured days before.

From these withdrawals it resulted that the British movements in either quarter were of no assistance to those in the other by direct co-operation, but only by diversion—by occupying in front of either flank a certain proportion of the enemy. The latter attempted no serious movement of attack, but simply waited. Their plan, alike in the strategy of the campaign and in the tactics of the battlefield, was to abide attack, with the advantages, usual to the defensive, of a carefully chosen position diligently improved. So placed and secured, they hoped to repel and to hold fast; but at the worst to inflict loss greater than they received and then to slip away successfully, avoiding capture, to another similar position in the rear of the first, there to repeat again the same tact For such retreat provision of horse mounts was always carefully made, and to its success their superiority in horseflesh, their habit of isolated movement, their knowledge of the country, and the friendliness of the inhabitants, greatly contributed. The student of naval history will easily recognise in these methods an analogy to the battle tactics plausibly ascribed to the French by Clerk in his celebrated treatise. It was often successful on the ground, but it did not win campaigns. The mastery of the sea remained with the British, whose blindly headlong attacks with their ships resembled in much the free and often foolish exposure of their troops in the beginning of the present war. Nevertheless, the temper is one which wins, nor is there any necessary incompatibility between a vigorous initiative and reasonable caution.

There is much to be said for such a plan as suited to the force numerically inferior, and especially when, as with the Boers, it is composed of men untutored in the military formations and manœuvres essential to successful movement in battle. Defence of the character indicated requires little change after the primary dispositions have been made; the men for the most part stand fast when placed, and do not incur the risk of confusion from which the well-practised only can extricate themselves.

The mistake of the Boers was in failing to recognise that a nation compelled to such a mode of action by its conditions of inferiority, in numbers and in drill, is doomed to ultimate defeat, unless at the very beginning, while the enemy has not yet developed or concentrated his powers, such an advantage is gained by a vigorous initiative as shall either prevent his obtaining the necessary initial positions, or shall at least postpone his doing so long enough to affect materially the course of the war, and give room for the chapter of accidents —for the intervention of the unforeseen. The Boers, having surprised their enemy at unawares, had the opportunity so to act. It may be that, had they done so, ultimate success would not certainly have followed— the odds were very great; but it is safe to say that only so, by rushing the campaign at the beginning, had they any chance of final victory. "Desperate conditions," said Nelson, "require desperate remedies." The Boers' position was desperate from the first, to be saved only by the most vigorous handling of numbers which for a brief and critical period were largely superior.

Thus it was that these opening weeks decided the character and issue of the war, beyond chance of subsequent reversal. By the Boers' own choice, interest was fixed not upon one or two, but upon several quarters, and these—save Ladysmith—determined not by their inherent, and therefore lasting and decisive, strategic importance, but by questions of commercial value and of the somewhat accidental presence in them of very small bodies of regular troops. At two places, Mafeking and Kimberley, the assailants were, as an English journal justly put it, "foiled by colonial forces hastily organised, and stiffened by small regular detachments which have shown far more enterprise on the offensive than their besiegers have done."

Such a situation, under the existing conditions of the general campaign, should have been met, not by protracted investment in force, but by assault; or, if that were inexpedient, a sufficient detachment should have been left to hold the garrison in check, while considerations of more decisive military importance elsewhere received concentrated attention.

Immediately after the arrival of Sir Redvers Buller he found the investment of the three garrisons—Ladysmith, Kimberley, and Mafeking—already accomplished. The question before him was complicated by the introduction of these new factors. As has before been said, it is generally understood that the expectation of the British authorities had been to proceed at once to an invasion of the Orange Free State, presumably by the line to Bloemfontein, with flanking movements on either side of it, while the forces in Natal were to stand simply on the defensive, until, by the advance of the army of invasion within supporting distance, the time for co-operation with it should arrive. In Natal, now, the tables were turned, the defence had broken down, and the army charged with it was shut up by a force so far superior as to enable it, not only to carry on the siege, but to make at least serious inroads upon the colony, if not to advance permanently to positions of more extensive control, to dislodge it from which greater effort would be needed. The question now to be decided was whether relief would be best effected by adhering to the original plan of moving in force upon Bloemfontein, leaving Ladysmith to look out for itself, and only strengthening the forces in Natal outside of the place sufficiently to check any further advance of the enemy; or whether to attempt speedier succour by a direct advance along the roads leading to one or both of the besieged places.

The first, if successfully carried out, would eventually take in the rear the assailants both of Kimberley and Ladysmith, threatening them with the severance of their communications—concerning which the Boers are exceptionally sensitive—and thus would raise the siege by compelling the retreat of the besiegers. This plan, moreover, would be faithful to general military principle, by keeping the great mass of the British Army concentrated upon a single object, and under a single hand.

The alternative possessed the drawback of dividing the army into two bodies virtually independent in their several movements, out of mutual supporting distance, and each distinctly weaker than the single mass intended for the great central operation of the former plan. The second also laboured under the other disadvantages that a direct advance naturally has as compared to a turning movement. The enemy would be met always in front—thus covering his communications and with retreat open—in positions assumed tactically with a view to prevent flank attacks and to compel assault in front, the most dangerous to make.

In choosing their ground for their objects, the Boers have shown remarkable aptitude. If overpowered and dislodged, unless routed and dispersed, the defender falls back continually upon the bases in his rear, recuperating his losses by reinforcements from them, while the victorious assailant must either press on with diminished numbers or must wait for reinforcements to come up, a delay that enables the defence still more to improve the next position, which, in a campaign of this sort, has commonly been selected long before. It may be said here that this was precisely the character of the advance on Kimberley about to be narrated. In such a direct operation, by its very nature, the defence gains strength and shortens his line of communications to be defended, while the reverse conditions unremittingly drain the powers of the assailant.

As an abstract military question there need be no hesitation in saying that the advance through the Orange Free State was in principle the correct plan, even under the existing conditions, as far as these are accurately known. But conditions are never accurately known to outsiders so immediately after a war. Even the hard bottom facts which ultimately appear, the residuum left after full publicity, and discussion, and side lights from all sources have done their work, do not correctly reproduce the circumstances as present to the mind of the general officer who decides. What is known now was doubtful then; what now is past and certain, was then future and contingent; what this and that subordinate, this force and that force could endure and would endure we now know, but who could surely tell six months ago? Who, whatever his faith in the heroism and patience of the garrisons, believed in December, 1899, that Ladysmith and Kimberley and Mafeking could hold out, without relief, as long as they did? What therefore, between the known uncertainties of the past and the certainly imperfect information of the present, we, who had not the responsibilities of decision, may modestly refrain from positively judging the particular decision, even by the generally sound principles which commonly govern such cases. Warfare is an art, not a science; it knows no unvarying laws, and possesses neither specifics nor panaceas.

Whatever the reason, the decision was reached to attempt simultaneously the relief of Kimberley and of Ladysmith. It is with the former, which also was first in order of time, that we now have immediately to do. This advance had begun, had reached its furthest limit, had been brought to a standstill, and so had failed, before the clash of arms at Colenso, on December 15, signalized the opening of the campaign for the relief of

Ladysmith. This priority was naturally to be expected; for not only was Cape Town the first port of arrival from England, but the much larger number of the besiegers at Ladysmith made a much longer time necessary to accumulate the force adequate to contend successfully against them. The details of the assembling of Methuen's division at Orange River Station need not detain us. The 2,500 men there in the first week of November had been increased by November 19 to nearly 10,000, and began to advance on the 21st. It will be well, however, to say a word about their objective, Kimberley, its conditions, its defences, and its defenders, as well as about the country through which runs the railroad that marks the general line of Methuen's proposed operation.

Lieutenant-Colonel Kekewich, who had been ordered to command the forces in Kimberley, had arrived there on the 13th of September. Already portions of the Transvaal levies were out, "on commando," as the Boer phrase is, moving on the Free State side of the boundary line; and many reasonably authenticated rumours were heard of intentions to destroy the railroad bridges—notably over the Modder and Orange Rivers—south of the place, as well as others north of it. The guard of the road generally was then in charge of a mounted body called the Cape Police, detachments of which watched the bridges. Political and other considerations prevented immediate steps from being taken to fortify the town, but plans were matured, and information concerning the surrounding country had already been procured by subordinate officers, whose arrival had preceded that of Kekewich. On the 18th of September, construction of defence works began, reports of movements by the burghers of the Free State as well as by Transvaalers being received, and arousing apprehension of a sudden attack. On the 27th of September, an officer of the garrison, by personal observation at Boshof in the Free State, ascertained that the burghers of the latter had been ordered out. The works were then pressed forward, and the formation of citizens into town guards already planned, was begun; 1,156 combatant members being enrolled, and placed under drill by non-commissioned officers of the regular battalion in garrison. The Boer forces continued to approach Kimberley, and on October 4, a week before war began, advanced bodies were within twelve miles. By October 7 the earthworks were so far forward that Kekewich considered the place practically safe against any attempt on the part of the enemy to rush it suddenly.

When the ultimatum expired, October 11, the garrison proper consisted of 570 Imperial and 630 colonial troops, for the defence of an unwalled town which contained 40,000 inhabitants and, being built in rambling fashion, had a very long circuit—about eleven miles—to be guarded. The ready co-operation of the citizens in military duty, both those already belonging to volunteer bodies and those not previously organised, but now enrolling themselves for the purpose, alone made the defence possible. From them, particularly, was formed a corps of irregular horse, which filled the want of mounted troops that at first was severely felt. Colonel Kekewich, recognising the enemy's overpowering superiority of numbers, rapidly drew into Kimberley all the outlying forces of every character under his command.

Although deeply concerned for the safety of the Modder River bridge, upon which in a measure would depend the advance of a relief column, "I was most anxious," he says, "that no disposition of troops made by me should give the enemy a chance of scoring a first success, even where the smallest body of British troops might be concerned. Taking into consideration that the enemy would probably not regulate his movements in accordance with the dictates of sound strategy, that he was in possession of mobile artillery in my immediate neighbourhood, I felt that if I had detached a small body of troops, necessarily without artillery, which it was not in my power to support from Kimberley, the enemy would in all probability concentrate very superior numbers, with artillery, against the small British post, and endeavour to destroy the troops composing the same. It was principally for this reason that I determined to concentrate all my available forces, including the Cape Police, at the point of greatest importance in my command—Kimberley."

The inference of Colonel Kekewich as to the Boers' strategy was as accurate as his general action was militarily judicious. The concentration and development of his resources not merely deterred the enemy from assault, but detained them there in force, to the neglect of matters elsewhere much more urgently worthy of their efforts. The gain of Kimberley, had they gained it, would have been poor compensation for the daily increasing solidity of the still weak British grasp on the central positions outlined by De Aar, Orange River and Naauwport. This absorption of the Boers' attention by Kimberley was maintained by frequent sorties of the garrison, in every direction, which at an early period of the siege became possible through the ready facility with which the citizens were converted into irregular mounted troops. "It will be observed," wrote Kekewich, "that portions of the mounted corps were employed on every occasion" of the continued sallies in greater or less force, especially at the period of Methuen's advance.

At the same time the enemy was preparing to bombard, and was busily engaged in taking possession, by small bodies of from 100 to 250 men, of the undefended towns and villages in Griqualand West—the thinly peopled district to the west of Kimberley. This pleasant but useless pastime occupied them agreeably, and diverted them from molesting the British at Orange River and De Aar.

"My general plan for the defence of Kimberley," says Kekewich in his report, "was based on the principle of always keeping the enemy on the move, and constantly in fear of an attack from an unexpected quarter. Later, when the advance of the relief column from the Orange River commenced, and I was put in possession of information concerning the probable date of its arrival in Kimberley, I adopted such measures as I hoped would cause the retention of a large force of the enemy in my immediate neighbourhood, and thus enable the relief column to deal with the Boer force in detail. It was with these objects that the numerous sorties and demonstrations in force were made by portions of the garrison of Kimberley."

Such continual offensive action is of the essence of dexterous defence, especially when designed in support of movements elsewhere occurring. It is not surprising, therefore, that Lord Roberts, in forwarding Kekewich's report, comments that "the greatest credit is due him for his able dispositions, for his rapid organisation of an auxiliary force, and for the tact, judgment, and resolution which he displayed throughout the siege." This admirable service was performed at a loss of 38 killed and 133 wounded, of all the troops employed from the beginning of the investment to the day of relief.

Orange River, where Methuen's relief force was assembling, is seventy miles from Kimberley. The country between is part of the great inland plateau, in general contour rolling, but with frequent stony hills, which locally have the name of kopjes, now become so familiar. These kopjes are of varying heights, from fifty to five hundred feet, and consist mainly of large boulders, with, however, a plentiful sprinkling of smaller rocks not too heavy for handling. The steepness and roughness of the surface make climbing a matter of hands as well as of feet, and are therefore a source of particular difficulty and exposure to an assailant; while, on the other hand, the broken heaps of huge stones afford to the defence much natural protection, and can be further improved by building shelter places, which it was the habit of the Boer to do, forming semicircular breastworks. In this way, with natural and artificial cover, was obtained a strong line of defence, depending in extent upon the length and formation of the kopje.

Superficial advantages at once strike the eye and impress the mind, and it was to the kopje therefore that the Boer first looked as the natural feature upon which to found his tactical and strategic scheme of offence. Its command over the plain country, by permitting fire tier above tier, compensated in part for any lack of development due to limited length or other causes, and afforded also several lines of defence to be successively occupied. But the height, while it imposes difficulties upon the attacker, has also drawbacks of its own. A downward, plunging fire demands definite precision and accuracy of aim, and in mark firing error in elevation is more commonly found than swerving to the right or left. The ordinary shot is more apt to fire over a man's head, or strike the ground ahead of him, than to miss him to one side or the other. When, therefore, it had been found by a few experiences—Talana Hill, Elandslaagte, Belmont and Graspan, in all of which the kopje bore a principal part in the scheme of defence—that the British soldier could not be stopped by them alone, the Boers, without abandoning the kopjes, reinforced them where the ground allowed by utilising the beds of the streams, which except in time of flood are nearly waterless. Men looking over the edge of a steep trench glance nearly along the ground in front of them, and if that be clear, unless they are singularly inexpert, their shots sweep along the surface so little above it that they are sure to catch men in front, so far as their height is concerned. This was done at Modder River, two-thirds of the way—forty-five miles—from Orange River, and also at Colenso; while at the disastrous battle of Magersfontein the Boers had strengthened one flank of their line by an artificial trench, which was backed by a kopje.

A peculiarity of the Boer tactical methods should here be described, originating in their habits of life and curiously adapted to the purely defensive scheme upon which they rely. Their aim is to consume the opponent's strength by compelling him to frontal attacks upon well covered men, who at the proper moment shall slip away, leaving the enemy an empty position and the prospect of another similar experience at each succeeding stage. To effect this, their horses were hobbled in the rear of the line, protected by the kopje, if one, or by such other means as offered; it is said even that many of the better to do, coming from a distance, would ride one horse to the place as to a hunting meet, and reserve a better and fresher for the retreat, which, in the earlier stages of Methuen's advance, was probably intended from the first. So far do they push the endeavour to leave a barren result to the victor that they carry away upon their horses, as far as may be and at some risk, not only their wounded but their dead; and of the latter those that cannot be removed are concealed. The singularity of this point of honour, and the tenacity of its observance, seem more congruous to primeval than to modern warfare.

The above description gives a general idea of the conditions confronting Methuen on the 21st of November, when he began his advance. In it he fought four actions: at Belmont, November 23; at Graspan on the 25th; at Modder River on the 28th; and finally at Magersfontein, December 11. These places are distant from Orange River, approximately, 18, 28, and 45 miles; Magersfontein being some three miles beyond the Modder.

The gathering of Methuen's division had not been unwatched by the Boers, and their forces, which, in two principal bodies of about 3,000 each, had been besieging Mafeking and Kimberley, and in other smaller detachments were scattered along the railroad between the two places, began to concentrate. On the 16th of October, 2,000 had occupied the Modder River Station. On the 10th of November a reconnaissance from

Orange River had found them occupying the ridges about Belmont, in numbers estimated at 700. At about the same time Kimberley noticed that the besiegers were increasing in numbers, while at Mafeking they were observed to be decreasing. On the 20th it was known that Cronje, whose reputation as a leader stood high, had been detached with his commando from before Mafeking, leaving it to the care of the local Boer troops, and going south. To these and other unrecorded movements of the same kind, all entirely correct in principle, are to be attributed the increasing numbers which Methuen encountered in his successive actions. It is to be remarked here that the Boers knew that inadequate transport material tied the British general to the railroad; and it was the continuance of this belief, when the difficulty had been obviated, that betrayed Cronje to his ruin at a later date.

Leaving Orange River on the early morning of Tuesday, November 21, the army, having rested during the extreme heat of the noons, camped on the evening of the 22nd within five miles of the enemy's position.

This was west of Belmont Station, and is described as a line of kopjes extending east and west, and about two hundred feet high. Lord Methuen's purpose in this and other actions was to cross the more dangerous open ground of the approach by dark, arriving at the foot of the kopjes before daylight. His line of advance being, in a general sense, parallel to the hostile front, it had been his intention that the left wing, after securing an eminence called Table Mountain on the enemy's right, should swing its own left around, performing a flanking, or else a general turning movement, pivoting upon the right wing. In the obscurity, however, the latter lost direction and the general found himself in consequence committed to a frontal attack. Orders were therefore sent to the left wing, which had not lost its direction, to conform its movements to those of the right, and the attack was delivered in front. The Boers are estimated to have been 2,000 to 2,500 men, the kopjes affording them three lines of defence in successive ridges.

Although the error in direction had necessitated a change in the method of attack, the time had been exact; the line had started at 3 A.M., reaching the foot of the hills before daybreak. This could scarcely have been much later than 4 A.M., for in the southern hemisphere summer was near. The musketry fire of the Boers opened soon after, "and the troops instinctively moved toward the enemy's position." The advance was covered by artillery, which, however, was slow in its movements, "the horses not having yet recovered from a five weeks' voyage." Criticism has said that the artillery was not sufficiently employed to silence the enemy's riflemen, but Lord Methuen alleges that shrapnel does not kill men in kopjes; "it only frightens them, and I intend to get at my enemy." The inferiority of shrapnel to shell, in use against kopjes, has been asserted by many observers. For these various reasons the battle of Belmont reduced itself to a magnificent charge by a much superior force up a stony and precipitous hill against an enemy strongly intrenched. "At 6.10 the last height was cleared, the enemy in large numbers galloping into the plain, their laager trekking across me 3,000 yards off, my mounted troops unable to carry out their orders on one side—left—because the retreat was covered by kopjes, and on the other—right—because too far ; the artillery dead beat and unable to help me. A cavalry brigade and a horse artillery battery from my right would have made good my success." The British loss at Belmont was 53 killed, 275 wounded ; that of the Boers is not accurately known.

Two days later at Graspan the Boers were in about the same force and the natural conditions similar in general character. The Boer line extended east and west, and at the latter end—their right—were "two high hills." These were bombarded with shrapnel, the effect of which was more thoroughly tested, one battery alone firing 500 rounds to clear the summit, before the infantry were allowed to advance. The men again fought their way to the top, but again the enemy got away. "The heights gained, I found I had taken the whole Boer force in flank, and had entirely cut them off from their line of retreat. My guns played on the masses of horsemen, but my few cavalry, dead beat, were powerless, and for the second time I longed for a cavalry brigade and horse artillery battery to let me reap the fruits of a hard-fought action." "The loss in both these actions," Methuen says, "was great, and convinces me that if an enemy has his heart in the right place he ought to hold his own against vastly superior forces, and it does our men great credit that nothing stops them."

Both actions, in short, illustrate the same lessons, the Boers' particular advantages for defence, their readiness in retreat, and, it must be added, the prompt facility with which they resorted to it. When the most that can be said has been said for their methods — and much can be said — it still remains that an eye ever to the rear, upon escape, is militarily a demoralising attitude upon which no sound system of warfare can be built up. The nervousness of the Boers at any seeming threat to their line of retreat has been so obvious as to elicit frequent comment. As a predominant motive it is ruinous.

The loss of the British at Graspan was

16 killed, 169 wounded. Lord Methuen noted in his report that he had fought distinctly different Boers on the two occasions. If he was not mistaken, this helps to account for the greatly increased numbers encountered three days later at Modder River. At Kimberley also it had been observed that the number of the besiegers was now much diminished, and a report, substantially correct, was received there that Cronje was marching south with 3,000 men. These, with the two bodies already fought, would bring the Boer force up to the 8,000 estimated by Methuen to be present at the next action, of November 28. The Kimberley garrison did not fail to occupy the attention of their besiegers by frequent sorties, one in considerable strength occurring on the day of the Modder River fight ; but such measures, however commendable, cannot beyond a certain point impose upon a sagacious commander with good information, and Cronje well knew that to stop Methuen was his principal affair.

The British force rested two days after Graspan, and at 4 A.M. of November 28 resumed its northward march. Methuen's information had led him to believe that the Modder was not held in force, and that he would meet his next serious opposition at Spytfontein, where the Boers would make their last stand ; the country between it and Kimberley, a dozen miles further on, being open and unfavourable to their defensive tactics. Reckoning upon this, he first intended, taking five days' rations, to make a circuit eastward by way of Jacobsdaal, crossing the Modder higher up, and coming in upon Spytfontein from that direction. The railroad, protected by earthworks, was to be left under guard of one or two thousand men. On the very eve of starting, intelligence came in that Modder River Station was strongly occupied, and the general, fearing under that condition to risk the railroad, decided to advance direct upon the river. He was still ignorant, and even unsuspicious, that the enemy had massed to the number of 8,000 to oppose the passage of the 7,000 to which casualties and the care of lengthening communications had reduced his own division.

The position taken by the Boers was on the south bank of the Modder, at the point where it is joined by the Riet. The two streams, flowing respectively from east and south-east, inclose an angle of forty-five degrees, the ground between them being called an island, though not so properly. The railroad crosses by a bridge—by this time destroyed—just below the junction; Modder River Station, a small, pleasant village, being on the north bank. In the approach from the south, by which the British were advancing, the land—or veldt—slopes evenly and regularly downward to the river, rising again beyond in such wise that the island is higher than the southern bank, but is in turn commanded by the northern.

Cronje had intrenched his riflemen along a line of three miles of the river bed, by which they were entirely concealed. On the island, which is covered with trees and brush, he had placed sharpshooters and quick-firing guns. On the extreme Boer right their position was further strengthened by broken, rocky ground and small kopjes, considerably in advance of their line. This forward cover they held by a strong detachment, as they did also another slight eminence, six hundred yards further east, upon which was a farm-house and kraal. From these a cross-fire upon the enemy served to protect their right flank, which by position otherwise was the weaker.

Although unconscious that he was about to encounter numbers equal to, if not greater than his own, Methuen, who expected them to retire after a show of opposition, considered it still his best course to advance with his two brigades on an extended front, the Guards on the right, the 9th Brigade on the left, the two carefully keeping touch from end to end and crossing in that order. Thus approaching, at 8.10 A.M. a very heavy fire showed that the river was held in force and caused numerous casualties, many men falling at once. "The Scots Guard Maxim detachment were completely wiped out." On the British right—Boer left—there was no break in the even slope of the ground, the Guards were visible for three miles from the river, and fully exposed alike to the fire of the trenches and that from the island; but the latter, without solid cover, was in turn closely searched by the British batteries, which, massed principally upon the right of their line, threw in the action over three thousand rounds. Under such heavy fire the Guards were directed to extend to the right, at the same time swinging round their extreme right companies toward the left. It was hoped thus to outflank and enfilade the hostile line; but the movement was checked by the Riet, which, contrary to the intelligence received, was not fordable. Colonel Codrington with a score of officers and men did get across; but the water was too deep for support to follow, and in returning some of the party were nearly drowned, having to hold hands to stem the force of the current. There was nothing for the right wing but to lie down when they had got within 1,100 yards of the enemy, and then patiently to await an outcome. Accordingly they thus remained from 10 A.M. until the sun went down at 6.20; the fire never ceasing, yet for all its intensity causing few casualties while the men lay quiet. "No one," wrote Methuen, in his report, "could get on a horse with any safety within 2,000 yards of the enemy." Under these conditions the conveyance of orders to different parts of the line was much embarrassed.

The left of the British front extended some distance west of the railroad. Here a rising ground, parallel to the river course, concealed the troops in their advance until its summit was reached, but there the same withering fire checked them. About 2 in the afternoon, however, two companies of light infantry succeeded by a rush in carrying the farm-house in front of the Boer lines, and almost at the same moment another detachment dislodged the enemy from the advanced kopjes on his extreme right. The parties thus established so threatened the Boers' flank as to shake their position.

An attempt was next made to gain and pass the river by a ford, which lies behind the farm-house, but this was too near the strength of the hostile fire and the effort was repelled. On their furthest left the British had better success. There the advanced kopjes supported the movement, and there the enemy's fire was weakest. A place deep but passable was found, and the Boers' right flank was turned under a heavy fire of infantry supported by a battery. First a party of twenty crossed, under Colonel Barter, of the Yorkshire Light Infantry—the names of all the men who do such a deed should be remembered, but their leader at least may be mentioned. Three or four hundred followed, and fixed themselves on the north bank, winning the outskirts of the village. Thence an advance of three-quarters of a mile up the river-side was made, the general of the brigade having now crossed; but this ground could not be held, and the British were forced back. Reinforcements were sent, and in performing this service Methuen's chief-of-staff, Colonel Northcott, was killed, the battle raging along the front in full severity. When the fire ceased at dark, the Boers still occupied their trenches, but the British were firmly settled upon their right flank and rear, on the north bank, and had possession of a practicable ford. During the night the Boers evacuated their positions, and the field of battle remained with the British, who continued to hold the line of the river up to the time that Roberts began his advance.

The battle of the Modder showed that, with the modern improvements in rapid-firing arms, it is possible for troops well entrenched over an extended front to sweep a plain field of approach with such a volume of fire as is impossible to cross. This it shows, but otherwise the lessons to be derived have been greatly exaggerated. Witnesses exhaust their descriptive powers to portray the evidences of the innumerable falls of bullets, shown by the kicking up of the dust. "A fire so thick and fearful that no man can imagine how any one passed under or through it. Many crippled lay flat for hours, not daring to rise for succour. If any one asked a comrade for a drink of water, he saw the bottle, or the hand passing it, pierced by a Dum-Dum or a one-pounder shell. If he raised his head to writhe in his pain, he felt his helmet shot away." *

The impression produced by the scene is most forcibly betrayed by the exaggerated phrase of the veteran commander in his first telegram—"One of the hardest and most

* Julian Ralph, "Toward Pretoria," p. 153.

trying fights in the annals of the British Army." Yet, as far as result was concerned, it was an immense expenditure of ammunition and little loss of life. The frontal attack was so clearly impossible that it was at once abandoned, and the men lay down. A generation or two ago they would have persisted, many more would have been killed, and while the position might at last have been carried in front, more than likely it would at the last have been turned, as it was at the Modder. The British loss, 70 killed, 413 wounded, was but 7 per cent. of the troops engaged—about 7,000—far below that of many of Wellington's battles.

In point of tactics, the battle may be summarized by saying that the British line held the enemy in front until a couple of detachments, by daring rushes, had established themselves in positions of command on the western flank, whence they worked themselves round, crossed the river, and fairly turned the hostile flank. And that, so stated, is a very old story. On the other hand, at Belmont and Graspan, at Talana Hill and Elandslaagte, it was shown that the same arms of rapid fire do not necessarily control where precision and skill, not mere torrential volume, are needed. Not only is it not demonstrated that modern weapons can stop the uphill advance of a resolute infantry on broken ground; it has been shown to probability that they are incapable of so doing. Whether such charges are wise is one thing, but whether they are possible is another. Rapidity of fire has reversed conditions where rapidity is the essential factor; it has not reversed them, probably not greatly modified them, where skill and resolution are chiefly demanded.

After the Modder fight Lord Methuen remained at the position then won, establishing a pontoon bridge, restoring that of the railroad, and awaiting reinforcements to replace the men lost in battle and those necessarily detached to protect his lengthening line of communications. After three severe actions he had now traversed forty-five of the seventy miles that lay between the Orange River and Kimberley; but the inadequacy of his numbers was increasingly felt. During the ten or twelve days at the Modder a serious demonstration was made in his rear at Enslin, threatening the railroad and his communications. Although successfully repelled, it was evident that the enemy's concentration had made them so far superior as not only to increase greatly his task in front, but also to threaten his rear. "The longer I remained inactive," said he, in his report, "the stronger would the enemy become. Therefore, on the day my last reinforcement arrived, I decided to continue my advance. It was out of the question to follow the railway, owing to the large kopjes on either side, which had been strongly entrenched. Besides, by that route there was not sufficient water."

The railroad, after crossing the Modder, runs on the west side of the river nearly due north for two miles, and then turns north-west for two more, when it passes between two kopjes, both fortified. The right-hand one of these, the Magersfontein, extends to the south-east for three miles, rising there to an abrupt peak about 150 feet high, which is the key of the situation. In the prolongation of this range a low ridge covered with brush extends eastward to the Modder, the bed of which thereabout follows for some distance a north-east and south-west line. At the foot of the peak, but some little distance in advance, the Boers had dug a line of trenches, which not only covered the immediate front, but at the eastern end of Magersfontein sweep round the curve of the hill to the north for some hundred yards, and then turned east again, following the bushy ridge to the river. These dispositions facilitated the passage of troops from one flank to the other under cover, and preserved control of a ford over the Modder behind the line. The trenches, especially before the peak, were filled with riflemen. The kopje itself was also manned, but it is allowable to believe that the experience of the war, already illustrated by many encounters, must have persuaded so shrewd a fighter as Cronje of the superior advantage of the trench system. Before the trenches ran a continuous line of barbed-wire fence. A probable estimate of the opposing forces places the Boers at 15,000, the British at 11,000. No certainty can as yet be predicated for the Boer numbers, which depend upon the enemy's calculations, but that they were decisively superior is scarcely doubtful.

After considering the problem before him, Methuen concluded that a turning movement was inexpedient. He could not, on the left, follow the railroad, for that was commanded on both sides. He could not, on the right, pass between Magersfontein and the Modder, for the bushy ground would prevent his artillery from helping him to its full power, and might even place it in danger of capture. If he deflected still more to the right, crossing the river, he would have to recross in the face of a force superior to his own in numbers and mobility. Moreover, in a circuit requiring time, he was hampered by the lack of transport which then fettered all British movements. He could take with him provisions for only five days. In any event he must fight again at Spytfontein; better therefore meet an enemy badly shaken by such determined assaults as those of Graspan and the Modder. Therefore, "I decided to attack the Magersfontein kopje." In this the main effort against the peak was assigned to the Highland Brigade, under General Wauchope, which had just joined. The force of this brigade was about 3,000.

On the afternoon of Sunday, December 10, the kopjes of Magersfontein were bombarded heavily, between 4.30 and 6.30 P.M., by a 4·7-inch gun from a distance of 7,000 yards. The Highlanders were directed to start a half hour after midnight, so as surely to reach the foot of the kopjes by daylight, due at 3.30 A.M. A drenching rain came on at 1, lasting through the night and adding greatly to the difficulty of keeping the direction, which was done by compass. This, however, was effected, though at the expense of much delay; but the danger of separating and struggling in the obscurity made it necessary that the troops should hold a compact formation, and they advanced in quarter column. The heaviness of the atmosphere postponed daybreak to 4 A.M. A few moments previously General Wauchope had given the order for deployment on the prearranged plan — one regiment moving ahead, two others to the right and left respectively, and a fourth forming in reserve. Some slight delay occurred, owing to local obstacles; and before the movement had developed, while the troops were still in mass and changing their places, a tremendous fire at two hundred yards opened from the line of trenches—every rifle apparently emptying its magazine as rapidly as the finger could handle the trigger. Coming wholly unexpectedly in the dark, at the critical moment of a change of formation, great confusion ensued, and contradictory orders were given, among which the most disastrous possible, "Retire," is said to have been uttered, causing a certain number to turn and break through the ranks behind them. In the final result the brigade, greatly shattered, lay down, and so remained for several hours.

Meanwhile the remainder of the army, with the exception of a small flanking force to the left of the Highland Brigade, took position on its right, prolonging the front in that direction to the Modder; some companies being thrown to the rear along the course of the river, guarding the fords against any attack of the enemy upon the right flank—demonstrations of which were made but repelled. The British artillery was brought actively and continuously into play, with perceptible effect upon the enemy's fire. The battle then resolved itself into both parties holding their positions until nightfall, when the Highland Brigade was withdrawn from the perilous position in which it had passed fifteen hours of exposure, heat and thirst. The British slept on the ground, their general purposing next morning to occupy the kopje, if deserted, but finding the enemy then still in the trenches, he withdrew his force to the Modder.

The battle of Magersfontein brought Methuen to a standstill, and postponed for more than two months the relief of Kimberley. The disaster which befell the Highland Brigade was one of those incidents which ought not to have occurred, but determination of blame must await more precise information than is now accessible. To retain the cover of darkness for an approach made within effective, though long, range of the enemy's fire—to deploy as near as possible to him, but still too distant to be seen—to keep 3,000 men in black darkness in touch, yet not compacted — these are conditions desirable of attainment but difficult to combine, and, like all combinations, liable to fail in some element. The total loss, by the last revised returns, was 171 killed, 691 wounded, four-fifths of which fell on the Highland Brigade and in the first few moments. Among the slain was General Wauchope.

From the day of this battle until February 11, the opposing forces continued in the positions occupied by them before the engagement, Methuen upon the north bank of the Modder, Cronje holding the ranges at Magersfontein and Spytfontein. The great comparative mobility of the Boers, with their more numerous and seasoned horses, enabled them to maintain the investment of Kimberley, and yet retain the power to concentrate be-times at any threatened point from this interior position. Here between the two bodies of the enemy, between Methuen and Kekewich, was the bulk of their army. Kimberley was never assaulted, nor did the inhabitants often see their enemy in any force.

During the same calendar week as Magersfontein, there occurred two other reverses—at Stormberg, December 10, and at Colenso, December 15—which made this the black week of the war for the British arms. These misfortunes, though chargeable in part to faulty dispositions upon the ground, and in part to the chapter of those accidents which have always to be allowed for in war, serve more especially to illustrate the embarrassments attendant upon the division of a force into two or more parts out of reach for mutual support, and neither one in decisively preponderant strength to the enemy to whom it is opposed. This disadvantage is greatest to the offensive, because to the defensive falls the privilege of increasing power by choice of position and by fortifying. It was in this dilemma that the British, in consequence of the abandonment of their original concentrative plan of advance through the Free State, and the adoption of two or more lines of operation, found themselves over their whole front; from Colenso on the east, through Sterkstrom and Naauwport, to the Modder River. The result throughout was—if not paralysis—at least a cessation of movement, after the reverses above mentioned, except in the brilliant and useful, but in scale minor, operations of General French upon their left centre, about Naauwport and Colesberg.

In the centre and east of the border district between Cape Colony and the Free State—from Naauwport to Stormberg and beyond—the position now was and continued to be especially critical, because most exposed. Had the Boer forces there been handled with definiteness of aim and concentration of effort in aggressive movement, serious disaster could scarcely have been averted. But direction seems to have been largely in the hands of the Free State farmers of the locality, whose aptitudes and leading carried them little above the level of irregular partisan troops. These are invaluable for their own purposes, but those purposes are distinctly subsidiary to war on the great scale, and by themselves alone do not decide campaigns. It is impossible not to be struck with the general similarity of motive, and of action, in the Boer operations from November to January in Cape Colony, from Stormberg to Dordrecht and thence to the Basuto boundary, and the dashing but militarily abortive raids to the rear of Lord Roberts' right flank while he was at Bloemfontein. As soon as the Dutch commandant in the latter instance settled upon Wepener for the expenditure of his strength, he had not only secured that opportunity for ready retirement to which the partisan looks, but he had also relieved the British commander from serious anxiety concerning his communications.

The British disaster at Stormberg possesses no intrinsic interest, or claim to mention, as a military incident; but as it attracted so much notice at the time, and carried a certain moral effect, the details must be summarized. The Dutch were strongly entrenched and in force on a hill overlooking the place. The British were at Putter's Kraal and Sterkstrom, some twenty odd miles distant by the railroad, which they controlled up to Molteno, nine miles from Stormberg. The troops, 2,500 in number, had been marching, or in open railroad trucks, since early morning of Saturday, December 9, when at 9 P.M. they detrained at Molteno.

From this place there are two country roads, one direct to Stormberg, the other branching to the left toward Steynsburg, on the Stormberg-Naauwport railway. General

Gatacre intended to follow the Steynsburg road for four or five miles, and there to take a turn to the right, which his guides assured him would in another mile and a half bring him to the south-west angle of the Boer position; but the turn was missed and passed, with the result that after a very long circuit, of two hours and a half, the column came out on the north-west angle. The attack was immediately delivered, but the troops, greatly exhausted, having halted only forty-five minutes since 9 o'clock, appear to have been incapacitated, by the accumulated hardships and disappointments of the night, to contend with the obstacles before them. The character of the casualties sufficiently indicates the comparative feebleness of the fighting. There were 31 killed, 58 wounded, while in prisoners there were lost 633. The accounts give the impression that many of the men taken were physically too depressed to quit the shelter in which they found themselves, in order to retire further. Two guns also were lost. The retreat which followed almost immediately was conducted under difficulties and fatigue, offering "great opportunity for an active enemy"; but it was not disturbed.

Further to the west and north General French, during this same period and the ensuing month of January, was carrying on continuous active operations, which will remain an instructive lesson for the military student, but which, from the smallness of the scale and the technical character of their merits, cannot well be related in a narrative of this character. For it he has received, if not popular appreciation, at least public reward in the high commendation of Lord Roberts, whose own achievements in a long career of honour give the greatest weight to his praise. "I consider that General French showed marked ability and judgment in constantly harassing the enemy and driving them from one strong position after another, without exposing his men to heavy loss." Yet even this scarcely measures the full value of French's services. The untiring molestation to which the enemy was subjected by him, as testified not only by his full report but by the daily telegram of this or that brush, first in one quarter, then in another, unquestionably

—or rather evidently—produced an impression and concentrated an anxiety that contributed to divert attention from the preparations to the westward, which were to result in the relief of Kimberley and the capture of Cronje. In these later events French was rewarded by the conspicuous as well as important part he played.

Reaching Cape Town immediately after the investment of Ladysmith, French was sent up country by Sir Redvers Buller with orders to seize Naauwport, then recently evactuated, and whenever possible to push on and gain Colesberg. Naauwport was reoccupied November 19, and thenceforth activity was incessant. Advancing, retiring, gaining, losing, on front, flank, or rear, of the enemy, whatever else found place, repose did not. The report is a record of unrestingness, which communicated itself to the enemy as uneasiness. On the 16th of December Arundel, midway from Naauwport to Colesberg, was occupied as headquarters, and from that time, as before, "every opportunity was taken to worry the enemy and to harass his flanks and rear until

December 29, when he finally evacuated his position in my front and retired on Colesberg. These operations were fully reported each night by telegraph." These telegrams journalise the restlessness of the skilled warrior who looks beyond his minor *rôle*—beyond mere partisan scurrying to and fro—to the great something to which he contributes.

Lord Roberts availed himself ably of the disquiet caused by French. As the fulness of time approached for the relief of Kimberley, the forces about Naauwport grew larger and more restless than ever. Advance in menacing force was made not only toward Colesberg, but to the eastward, along the railroad to Steynsburg and Stormberg. Parties of colonial horse crossed the country from Gatacre at Sterkstrom to French and Kelly-Kenny at Steynsburg and Arundel. A general advance in force seemed imminent. On February 2 French, in closing his long report to Lord Roberts detailing the events since December 16, said, "In accordance with the instructions received at Cape Town from the commander-in-chief, I am now making the arrangements ordered." The explanation of this mysterious allusion appeared thirteen days later, when, on February 15, he led the relieving column into Kimberley, two hundred miles distant. The same day his former command, weakened by his own withdrawal with the cavalry, and by that of Kelly-Kenny's division, and now under General Clements, had been forced out of Arundel by greatly superior numbers; but to what avail? Yet in another ten days the Boers from Kimberley to Colesberg were in full retreat, and on February 26 Clements not only had regained his ground, but had entered Colesberg, for which French had so long manœuvred in vain. The incident illustrates happily the far-reaching effect of a great movement in mass, wisely conceived, ably directed, and secretly executed.

CHAPTER V

THE NATAL CAMPAIGN FROM THE INVESTMENT OF LADYSMITH THROUGH THE BATTLE OF COLENSO

THE severing of communications, by rail and telegraph, between Ladysmith and the outer world, was the first step in a preliminary process of attack and of defence; after which only the opponents settled down to the relatively permanent conditions that constitute the monotonous endurance of a siege. The British, prior to accepting the investment, struck out right and left from day to day, by skirmishing and reconnoitring parties; the Boers on the 9th of November delivered an assault described as determined in character, which will be more particularly mentioned later, but concerning which details are singularly meagre. This no doubt is owing, partly, to the habitual reticence of the Boers concerning their reverses, and partly to the isolation of the British garrison and correspondents until a time when nearer and more exciting events engrossed the columns of the press, crowding out this affair, already become past history.

Unless the author has greatly misconceived the general utterances, the occupation of Ladysmith has been in popular estimation merely an unfortunate accident forced upon the British as a result of the original faulty dispositions of the campaign. This view is scarcely correct; and even if it were in part well founded, the natural inference, that the investment was a misfortune, pure and simple, would not follow. Probably no single incident of the war has been more determinative of final issues than the tenure of Ladysmith. Therefore, an examination of the relation borne by this single factor to the whole, of which it was a part, may very fitly precede immediately the narrative of the particular occurrences which locally centred around it.

The considerations of any and every nature which made Ladysmith a railroad junction, a cross-roads, at which met three important lines of communication—one with Durban, one with the Transvaal, and one with the Orange Free State—constituted it at the same time, necessarily and consequently, a position of strategic importance. Even had a mistake been made in selecting it as a railroad centre—which I have never seen asserted — the decision alone would have given it value; but, if the choice was sound, all the considerations which dictated it go to increase that value. It does not follow, of course, that such a position must under no circumstances be abandoned, that something better than its tenure might not have been done for the British campaign; still less is it to be concluded that the only, or the best, way to hold the place was by occupying the town itself, or the particular lines ultimately established around it by Sir George White.

These are questions of detail, which, however important, are separable in thought and in decision from the general fact stated —that Ladysmith, being a railroad crossing, the only very important one on the Natal theatre of operations, was necessarily a strategic point not lightly to be surrendered.

Nor was Sir George White, in deciding to hold the place, constrained only by the demands of an immediate emergency. The thoughts and reasonings of that gallant and distinguished officer have been sequestrated from public knowledge by the same causes that obscure most of the early happenings of the siege; but, from speeches made by him shortly after his return to England, it is clearly apparent that not only a present military exigency, but also the considerations above mentioned, were present in his mind, as indeed they could not fail to be with any instructed and intelligent officer. "Natal was the object on which the Boers had set their hearts. It was not only the actual point which they attacked, but it was also their sentimental object. They had the idea that they had a right in Natal, and their plan of campaign was framed from the very idea that they should have the territory from Majuba to the sea. But Ladysmith stood in their way, and he might say that Ladysmith was a most important town in northern Natal. From its geographical position it became of great strategical importance. It was at Ladysmith that the forces of the Transvaal, pouring over the northern and north-eastern passes of Natal, first joined with the forces that came in from the west and the Orange Free State, and there the two South African Republics combined in their strength under the late Commandant-General Joubert—a man who, he would like to say there, was a brave and a very civilised man. Ladysmith was also a railway centre of great importance, and it was therefore of great value to them to keep it out of the possession of the enemy." *

Nor was this all, as touching the place itself. That similar reasonings had led the Imperial authorities, antecedent to the hostilities, to choose Ladysmith as a depot and *place d'armes*, is shown by the reproaches addressed to the Government by the London *Times*, November 21, 1899: "There is no need to inquire just now into the balance of political and military considerations which determined the policy of making a stand at Ladysmith. It is enough that that policy was definitely adopted in ample time to allow of providing Ladysmith with the long-range guns which

* London *Weekly Times*, May 18.

its position renders peculiarly necessary, dominated as it is by hills on three sides. Why were such guns not provided? Why was it left to fortunate accident to furnish the garrison at the very last moment with the means of defence"—by the arrival of the naval guns?

In like manner the prime minister of Natal, some months later, challenged the following statement of the *Times* in its issue of March 2, 1900: "From November 2, when, owing to the subordination of military to local political considerations, a British force of 10,000 fine soldiers was shut in Ladysmith, a great fear has hung over us." Upon this the premier comments: "It is true that the Governor, when asked by Sir George White to give his opinion, pointed out the serious political consequences which might follow the evacuation of Dundee. But as far as Ladysmith was concerned the abandonment or evacuation of that town was never, to my knowledge, even hinted at. For two years or more previous to the outbreak of the war, Ladysmith had been made the principal military station in Natal; large quantities of commissariat stores and ammunition had been accumulated there; and the troops stationed at Ladysmith, comprising the larger portion of the Natal garrison, had been permanently hutted instead of being retained under canvas. Of one fact I am certain, and that is that no suggestion of any kind was ever made to the Government of Natal that, for military or any other reasons, it was undesirable that Ladysmith should be defended."

Intrinsically, therefore, Ladysmith presented strong claims, inherent and acquired, against abandonment. But there were further reasons, exterior to herself, to be found in the particular condition of the military problem. In all campaigns, and especially in those which are defensive in character, as this then was, it is an accepted principle that the front of operations should be advanced, or, in case of retreat, should be maintained, as far forward as is possible consistent with general considerations of safety. Prominent among the latter is always the securing of the lines of communication, by which alone supplies and reinforcements can be received, or further retreat made in case of necessity. By detaining the enemy in such an advanced position, security—partial or total—is obtained for the various interests in the rear, whether public or private. The question of such detention, however, if to be effected by an inferior army, is difficult and complicated; for which reason, as well as because of other disadvantages inherent in inferiority, a defensive campaign really great—great, that is, in a military sense—makes the highest demand upon military skill.

It was the defensive stage of Napoleon's Italian campaign of 1796 that illustrated his greatness, even more conspicuously than the offensive movements which preceded it, extraordinary exhibitions though they were of his military genius; and the same distinction attends his resistance of the allied invasion in 1814.

In certain conditions of country, in certain relative degrees of numerical strength, under certain political conditions—for it is a grave mistake to think that military and political considerations can be dissevered practically, as they can logically—an inferior force can contest step by step, content to delay only, not to arrest. It is, for instance, evident that, politically, one may more readily thus abandon hostile country than uncover one's own territory—as in Natal—even though the military conditions in the two cases be identical. But, under different circumstances of position or of numbers, such dilatory field operations may be impracticable. If the country through which retreat is to be made be open, if numbers be so small that the enemy can overlap—that is outflank—if the ground does not afford positions where the flanks may be protected by natural obstacles that make outflanking impossible or exceedingly arduous, if the enemy be greatly superior in mobility, in such conditions retreat from each successive stand is apt to be precipitate—dependent less upon one's own will than upon the enemy's energy—and the retiring army may reach its ultimate goal under an accumulation of retrograde impulse not far distinguishable from rout, deteriorated in *morale* and diminished in numbers.

Where such unfavourable conditions obtain, the principle which dominates all correct defensive action receives a special application. The principle is that every defensive disposition should look to offensive action—or at the least to offensive effect. Mere defence is ultimate ruin. "In the long run," said Napoleon, "no position whatever can be defended if it does not threaten the enemy." * Consequently, the force that for any, or several, of the reasons above given cannot safely keep the field must establish itself solidly in some place where, for whatsoever advantages, it is as far as possible itself secure; but whence at the same time—and this is the more important of the two considerations—it most effectually menaces the enemy. This it does by applying again, but in another manner, the flanking, or turning, idea — by placing itself across or to one side of the line of communications upon which the enemy will depend, if he ventures to advance in the direction which the defendant has not felt himself strong enough otherwise to contest.

* I should greatly like here to take up my parable against those who base their calculations for the numbers and kinds of naval vessels upon the idea of "a navy for defence only"; but space and relevancy both forbid.

Of such offensive-defensive positions there are many historical examples. Among these the most recently conspicuous was the occupation of Plevna by the Turks in 1877, and the long consequent arrest of the Russian progress; but Mantua, in 1796, in like manner and for the same reasons, effectually stopped Bonaparte for eight months, and Genoa, in 1800, so long delayed the Austrians as to reverse the issues of the campaign signalised by the name of Marengo.

From the simply defensive point of view, a line of works arranged consecutively around such a stationary centre has no flanks to be turned, but resembles a circle or other continuous curve which returns into itself. Like a straight line, such a curve may be broken by superior force; but until that is done the weakness of flanks does not exist. Moreover, succour can be more quickly sent from a centre to every threatened point of the circumference than from the middle of a line of equal length to its extremes. A circle, therefore, is the most compact disposition for defence, and so most ideal for smaller numbers. It is concentration in its most effective form, while sacrificing nothing in elasticity and flexibility of motion.

These are the intrinsic defensive advantages —as distinguished from the offensive threat to the enemy's communications—secured to the weaker party by a permanent position, and these are its compensations for the loss of open communications which have been deliberately abandoned.

In Natal, at the end of October, 1899, the British army was much inferior to the enemy in both numbers and mobility; and while several lines of defence were to be found in the region behind, as was shown by the stubborn resistance which the Boers, when in turn outnumbered, made at the Tugela, these positions were open to the danger of being turned by superior numbers or superior rapidity; still more when these two were combined. In fact, much of the subsequent Boer success in defence resulted from the fact that, acting on the inside of an arc, with the advantage of interior—shorter—lines, they also moved over the latter with greater speed, owing to their distinguishing characteristic as mounted troops. They had particular facilities, in a word, for accumulating successful numbers at a threatened point of a stationary defence, which the British would not have had in an active campaign of retreat.

It became therefore advisable, if not imperative, for the British commander in Natal to resort to a stationary defence for the preservation of his division, and to place himself for offensive purpose upon the flank of the enemy's possible line of invasion, in order to deter him from further advance. As to situation, Ladysmith was clearly indicated by the reasons before stated, and especially because there was there accumulated a great quantity of ammunition, provisions, and other supplies, which not only should not be allowed to fall into the hands of the Boers, but also would be essential to the maintenance of the garrison, if relief were long delayed, as it proved to be. That this contingency was foreseen, and as far as possible provided for, has been shown by subsequent utterances of Sir George White. "From the moment I saw the situation in Natal, I was certain I should be pressed back by superior numbers, and have to hold Ladysmith, and I knew that the enemy had guns with which I could not hope to cope with my 15-pounder field guns. Therefore I telegraphed for the naval guns. It was a question of a race for them, and Captain Lambton was the right man to win that race. He won only by a short head." *

This, then, was the function which the current of events assigned to Ladysmith, and the part which it bore to the subsequent development of the war. Discussion has been thus long because, in the author's judgment, White's action in shutting himself up in the place, and the admirable tenacity of himself and of the garrison in their resistance, were the shaping factors in a contest the ultimate result of which was probably certain in any event, but which in feature and occurrence would have been very different had Ladysmith either not been occupied or proved incapable of protracted resistance. As so often markedly happens, when a correct

* London *Weekly Times*, June 1, 1900. Captain the Hon. Hedworth Lambton, Commander of the "Powerful," accompanied the naval guns to Ladysmith, and was there throughout the siege.

decision has been made, circumstances seemed to work together to favour the consequences. The respite given to the garrison by Joubert, who did not attack until November 9, allowed opportunity to regularize and further to develop the system of defence, so that on November 6 a press censor telegram, brought out successfully by a Kaffir runner, read, "Position here now believed to be entirely safe; greatly strengthened in the last twenty-four hours." The opportune arrival of the naval guns also, though by so narrow a margin of time, decisively influenced the outcome. "Had it not been for these guns," said Sir George White, after his return to England, "the guns of the Boers would have been brought up very much nearer to my defences of Ladysmith, and it would enormously have embarrassed my powers of resistance and would have added enormously to the mortality of my garrison. Not once or twice in our rough island story have the naval officer and his men come in the nick of time, and the siege of Ladysmith was but one instance added to these happy advents."

As before said, Ladysmith is surrounded on three sides by hills which overtop it; railroad lines and stations, indeed, do not commonly prefer summits to valleys. On the 30th of October the Boers had already mounted a 40-pounder gun on Peppworth's Hill, north of the town, with which on that day they opened fire at a distance of over 6,000 yards, much outranging the army field artillery. It was in connection with the general sortie of the garrison to seize that position that the disaster of Nicholson's Nek was incurred.

This first threatening outlook was materially modified by the arrival the same day of the six naval guns from Durban, two of which were of power equal to the Boers' heavy pieces, and all of a range superior to those previously at White's disposal. By the 3rd of November a second long gun had been placed by the besiegers some 8,000 yards—between four and five miles—south-east of the town, upon Mount Umbulwani; from which, and from an eminence known indifferently as Lombard's Kop and as Little Bulwana, three miles to the northward, and also east of the place, the worst of the heavy gun fire upon the town itself, as distinguished from the lines of defence, seems to have proceeded. On the 28th the Boers had established within 5,000 yards—less than three miles—of the western defences a third 40-pounder, to which, we learn from Joubert's despatches, his gunners with grim military humour gave the name of "Franchise"—in mockery, doubtless, of the British Government's demands on behalf of the Uitlanders. It may be mentioned here that throughout the war the Boers have shown a remarkable facility in transporting these heavy cannon, placing them with surprising rapidity in positions unexpected by their opponents. On the 29th the besieged could count twenty-six guns in place upon the lines of attack; but of these, at that time, only the three specified were guns "of position," to be reckoned as units of a siege train. The British defensive works, when finally established, measured in circuit some sixteen miles. The range of the heavier hostile guns, as revealed by their early practice, compelled an extension to this degree, in order to hold them back beyond easy command of the town. Fortunately this perimeter, which would indicate the enclosed area to have a diameter of from five to six miles, could be manned without overtaxing the numbers of the garrison. At the moment of investment the British force fit for duty was 572 officers and 12,924 men; total, 13,496. Of these, during the siege, 88 officers and 732 men were killed or wounded; but sickness and want of food had so far further reduced the numbers that on the day of relief there were of effectives only 403 officers and 9,761 men, and of these it was significantly added that "they are the only troops fit to do even a two-miles march." *

Long before this condition of destitution and debility was reached the besiegers found their hands so occupied by the British relieving forces that the besieged had little more to do than to hold on. When the danger to Ladysmith had decided the British authorities to depart from the original plan, of a single forward movement in mass through the Free State, and to organise instead a double advance,

* London *Weekly Times*, April 27, 1900. Some other interesting siege statistics will be found in the same number.

with divided forces, for the simultaneous relief of Ladysmith and of Kimberley—as well as certain other subsidiary operations by French and Gatacre—heavy reinforcements were at once directed upon Natal. Hildyard's brigade, which had left England before the news of Talana Hill was received, went on at once from Cape Town without disembarking, reaching Durban before November 17. Lieutenant-General Sir Francis Clery continued on to the same port from his original destination, Port Elizabeth, and upon arrival, November 18, took command of all the forces in the colony south of Ladysmith. He was followed exactly a week later by the Commander-in-Chief, Sir Redvers Buller, drawn in person by the irresistible logic of events to the scene which his own action, or that of the Government, had determined to be the chief among several centres of active operations.

Meantime, since the day of investment, much had been happening, and conditions were rapidly taking shape. Upon the 9th of November Joubert directed an attack upon the defences of Ladysmith. This delay of a week has not yet been explained, and is to be justified only upon grounds of necessity, in the Boer commander's inability, however occasioned, sooner to get his numbers together, concentrated and disposed for so grave an enterprise. The solution is probably to be found partly in his own natural temperament, which his previous career, though political rather than military, indicates to have been cautious, and lacking in the aggressive quality that has given President Kruger, in civic contests, a continuous triumph over his more cultivated and progressive, but less combative, rival.

It is to this trait of wariness, seeking to compass ends by indirection and compromise rather than by open conflict, that Joubert's failure to achieve success in public life has been plausibly attributed, and from it arose the nickname "Slim (crafty) Piet" attached to him by his countrymen. "It was this want of assertiveness and of determination in following any marked line of action which prevented Joubert from playing a great part in the fortunes of the Republic. Opportunities occurred again and again after the advent of the Uitlanders when a vigorous assertion of himself would have placed him in a position to defeat Mr. Kruger. But the habit of indolence, so often found associated with a big physical frame, and a certain element of Scotch 'canniness,' which led him to refuse to accept risks, prevented his offering serious opposition to the Kruger clique."

This estimate of Joubert's characteristics is recently confirmed by two sympathetic observers from within the Boer lines. "Mr. Davitt, in a letter from Kroonstad to the Dublin *Freeman's Journal*, declares that the Boers were not at all dismayed by the death of General Joubert, which they agreed was in no sense a misfortune. He was too merciful in his notions of warfare. Ladysmith could easily have been taken on more than one occasion had Joubert not vetoed the proposed assaults." * The second correspondent relates that General Joubert overruled the desire of the burghers to assault Ladysmith, saying "at a War Council that the city was not worth to the Boers the lives of 500 burghers." If Joubert really said that, he ought unquestion-

* London *Times*, June 25, 1900.

ably to have been at once relieved from command; but as the incident is preceded by the statement that "the burghers were confident of their ability to take it in a hand-to-hand fight, *notwithstanding that the English outnumbered them more than two to one*,"* the source of the correspondent's information is open to some question.

To make war without running risks—not mere risk of personal danger, but of military failure—has been declared impossible by the highest authority. Yet such a temperament, betrayed in politics, being constitutional, will enter into all actions of life, and one is not surprised to read that "this characteristic of caution was the chief mark of Joubert's conduct in the field as a military commander. His idea of warfare was to act ever on the defensive." Let this be qualified so far as to say that his idea appears always to have been to act within limits of safety, to consider self-preservation—the preservation, that is, of his own forces—more important than the destruction of the enemy, and we have a view, not of Joubert only, but of his race, which

* *Harper's Monthly Magazine*, July, 1900, p. 174.

goes far to explain the failures at Ladysmith, Kimberley, and Mafeking, and likewise the inefficient action at that early period of the war when alone success was locally possible, and, if locally attained, might have even compassed an ultimate victory. If to this idea be linked that which is closely akin to it—of attaining results, not by superior dexterity in the use of means, but by subtlety and ambush —and we have the explanation both of the numerous artful traps into which British detachments were led, like game into the snare of the hunter, and yet also of the sure failure to achieve success in war, for the craft of the hunter is not the skill of the warrior.

The cognate words "stratagem" and "strategist" sufficiently indicate that craft and wile are part of the professional equipment of great warriors, but with them these are not, and cannot be, predominant. Their skill is not so much to contrive success by deceiving an enemy as to command it by local superiority of force, either exerted in violence, or imposing submission by mere evidence of overpowerment. Circumvention with them aims at permanent results which it alone cannot obtain.

It is but a means to the end, which is the crushing, the military annihilation, of the enemy. That can be accomplished only by force, not by mere guile. In his temperament, as shown by his action, Joubert reflected the fighting characteristics of his people, of whom he has been the most conspicuous military representative, honoured by friend and foe alike for his fearlessness, his intelligence, and his humanity. Courage of the highest proof as regards personal danger, but not the courage that throws away the scabbard, much less that which burns its ships. The hunter, meeting superior strength with superior cunning, without even the very least willingness to lose his life in order to carry his end, may be brave even to recklessness; but he rejects habitually the tone of mind distinctive of the soldier, who counts life naught if only by its sacrifice the end may be attained, or honour preserved. In so far, that element of stupidity which has been somewhat lavishly attributed to the British officers' too single-minded attention to their end, to the exclusion of care for their own persons and those of their men, has a military value not only great, but decisive.

The quality needs direction and control, certainly; but, having been reproached for now two centuries, the question is apt—Where has it placed Great Britain among the nations of the earth?

The assault of November 9 began, as is usual in such cases, with a heavy artillery fire, intended to shake the endurance of those subjected to it. The Boer guns opened at 4 A.M., and under their cover the assailants moved forward. The attack was made from all sides, but the principal effort came from the northward, between the railroads leading north-east to Glencoe and north-west to the Free State. As before said, particulars are wanting; but the British had only to hold their own, except when by a rush, after a repulse of the enemy, they gained ground over which the latter had passed; whereas the Boers, having to break cover frequently in order to advance, underwent necessarily the greater burden of exposure and of loss. How large this was is still uncertain. Sir Redvers Buller, on the 5th December, telegraphed to the War Office that it was "very difficult to make any statement as to the enemy's losses. For instance, at Belmont, 81 of their dead were accounted for; they gave 15 as the number of killed. There is every reason to believe that in the fight at Ladysmith, on November 9, the enemy's loss was over 800 killed and wounded." The Boer practice of removing or concealing their slain has already been noted. The British casualties on this occasion were at the time reckoned at about 100. Whether subsequent estimates materially changed this figure is not particularised; but probably it is nearly correct, for the total losses during the investment, exclusive of the great assault of January 6, were only 355. The enemy were effectually repulsed all along the line, and the fighting was mostly over by 11 A.M. At noon a salute was fired, in honour primarily of the Prince of Wales's birthday; but, incidentally, doubtless, it expressed exultation over the garrison's own achievement.

Nearly two months elapsed before the attempt to carry the works by storm was renewed, and then, doubtless, because it had been recognised that there was at least a dangerous probability that the place might hold out, until it was relieved by the immense forces known to be accumulating. But the immediate result of the failure of the 9th was to dispose the Boer authorities not to risk further slaughter, but to trust rather to the slow process of famine for overcoming an endurance which neither they, nor probably the British outside, then thought could be so long protracted.

Joubert therefore settled down to an investment and bombardment. Immediately following this determination, and probably consequent upon it, there were organised a number of raids upon the Natal territory to the southward. These, though simultaneous in execution, and therefore mutually supporting, were made by bodies apparently individually independent; sharing in this a characteristic commonly met in the Boer operations, and facilitated at once by their individualistic habits of life, their knowledge of the country, and their freedom from the organic interdependence which to regular troops becomes a second nature. Every Boer organisation seems susceptible of immediate dissolution into its component units, each of independent vitality, and of subsequent re-union in some assigned place ; the individuals passing easily as innocent wayfarers or peasants among the population, with which they readily blend. The quality has its strength ; but it has also its weakness, and the latter exceeds. This capacity for undergoing multifold sub-division, with retention of function by the several parts, is characteristic, in fact, of the simpler and lower forms of life, and disappears gradually as evolution progresses to higher orders. In all military performance, it is not the faculty for segregation that chiefly tells. It is the predisposition to united action, the habit of mutual concert and reliance. By this, concentration of purpose, subordination to a common impulse, ceases to be an effort, becoming the second nature of the man ; and concentration of action, not merely in great operations but in the inner spirit, is the secret of success in war. Individual, intelligent self-direction is not, however, thereby excluded. The two are complementary elements of the highest personal efficiency ; but they must be regarded in their due relations and proportions. The individualistic tendency is that of the natural man, of the raw material, of the irregular trooper. Educated in the trained soldier into due subordination to the superior demands of military concert, it remains an invaluable constituent of military character; but where existing in excess, as it does prior to training, it is far more harmful than beneficial In considering the experiences of a war of the kind before us, these facts should be kept clearly in mind; for under the peculiar conditions of countries partly or wholly unredeemed, as the American wilderness of a century or so ago, or South Africa to-day, the special experience of the inhabitant confers local aptitudes which the trained soldier needs to acquire, which place him for the moment, and in so far, in a position of inferiority, and in consequence of which hasty impression lightly reaches the erroneous conclusion that greater military efficiency resides in individual liberty of action, than in imposed habits of subordination and concert of movement. It is not so. The exception should not be mistaken for the rule, nor the occasional for the permanent.

Incidentally to the process of investment, the Boers had already moved in considerable numbers south of Ladysmith, and had established batteries on Grobler's Kloof, a ridge two or three miles west of the railroad, overlooking the Tugela from the north. Thence they had opened fire on the 2nd of November against Colenso, the town and railway station upon the southern bank, and against Fort Wylie, upon the northern, just to the east of the road. Colenso and Wylie were consequently evacuated by the small British forces there present, and on the 4th it was announced officially that they had retired to Estcourt, twenty miles to the southward — twenty-seven by the railroad. This marked the furthest point of the British retreat; but the fewness of the troops that there made their stand exposed them for some days to very serious danger, had the object of the Boers been, as was by some alleged, with firm purpose to destroy whatsoever of force or of facilities existed to further the advance of relief to the invested garrison, and not merely raiding with a view to increase their resources in the positions they had determined to hold, around Ladysmith and on the Tugela.

Up to the 15th of November an armoured train was sent out daily from Estcourt to reconnoitre, but on that day, having pushed too far north, it was intercepted on its return by an advanced party of the enemy, who, by loosening a rail, threw it off the track. A hundred British, more or less, were here captured; among them Mr. Winston Churchill, a war correspondent. Three days later, November 18, there were seen from Estcourt the advanced patrols of the various raiding parties, who were sweeping the country on both sides of the railroad over a front of thirty miles or more, from Weenen on the east to Ulundi on the west. On the 21st they were reported in the direction of Greytown, forty miles east of Estcourt and the same distance from the railroad, which here runs south-east, and also at Impendhla, twenty-five miles west of the road. Their advance was pushed close to the Mooi River, which the railroad crosses twenty miles to the southward of Estcourt, and there artillery shots were exchanged with the camp where

Sir Francis Clery was assembling the reinforcements arriving at Durban—the beginnings of the force destined to the relief of Ladysmith.

Communication of Estcourt with Mooi River was for a short while interrupted, both by rail and by telegraph, the enemy occupying Highlands Station, thirteen miles to the southward, on the 20th, and also a position commanding Willow Grange, midway between Highlands and Estcourt. At no time, however, did the Boers make any serious demonstration, looking towards the permanent isolation of the place; nor was there any attempt to capture it. The whole movement, as it resulted, was simply a raid, and nothing more, with no apparent objects except to secure supplies, and, while so engaged, to insure their own safety from molestation by occupying positions of command, which facilitated their defence and—by menace or otherwise—imposed obstacles upon the movements of the British. A certain amount of outpost skirmishing of course occurred, and on the night of the 22nd some 4,000 British, under General Hildyard, moved, by way of Willow Grange, to attack Beacon Hill, which overlooks Estcourt from the west. The Boers were in force there, and upon still higher ridges farther to the westward. A sharp engagement took place that night, in which the British first carried the position, but afterwards retired, leaving it to be reoccupied by the enemy. The movement on their part seems to have been simply precautionary, a sharp rap to check the over-confidence of the opponent, and to deter him from pushing attacks upon the railroad, which for the time being might be inconveniently successful; the reinforcements from Durban having as yet only partially come up, and the organisation for advance being still incomplete. The British loss was 11 killed, 67 wounded.*

No attempt on a large scale was made to arrest the Boer raiding operations. From this, and from their mutually independent character, it has resulted that the numbers engaged in them have remained very uncertain, not having been observed or tested by the usual military methods. By one correspondent

* The latest revised official returns of casualties now (July 18) accessible to the author are to be found in the London *Times* of July 4, and are complete to June 30.

on the spot they were estimated at not over 5,000;* by another, equally present, at from 7,000 to 12,000.†

Sir Francis Clery had apparently determined to concentrate his entire effort upon organising the relief of Ladysmith, and was not to be drawn off by side events, however disastrous to local interests. The British force at Estcourt and at Mooi River were considered safe, and the enemy's advance in fact did not extend in any force beyond the latter. Very shortly after the affair at Willow Grange the tide began to ebb. The precise cause for this is still a matter of surmise. It may be that Joubert considered he had gathered in all that was needed to supply his positions around Ladysmith and behind the Tugela; it was reported at the time that 12,000 head of cattle were among the spoils. It may be that he found the British force, although yet only partially concentrated and organised, too strong to justify a more extended movement. It had been rumoured that he purposed to capture, if possible, Estcourt and Mooi

* Atkins, "Relief of Ladysmith," p. 117.

† Burleigh, "Natal Campaign," p. 127.

River, and even to push on to Pietermaritzburg, with the view of stopping the relief column as far as possible from its point of destination. Such an effort was strictly accurate from the strategic standpoint, and accordingly his whole movement may have been of the nature of a reconnaissance in force, to receive greater development if circumstances favoured, and in any event to impose delay by destroying the roads. To this, however, it must be replied, even in the ground covered, the injury to the rail, though often attempted was nowhere serious, except where culverts or bridges offered vulnerable points.

Another interesting and far from improbable story was current at the time, that Joubert's retirement was due to peremptory orders from Pretoria, elicited by the progress of Methuen, the operations around Naauwport, and the increase of British force in that central region which French's movements, and those of Gatacre before Stormberg, seemed to indicate. This report is mentioned by two correspondents then at Estcourt,* as based upon despatches

* Burleigh, "Natal Campaign," p. 128, 129. Atkins, "Relief of Ladysmith," p. 116.

captured on Boer couriers on November 25, directing Joubert to return at once to Ladysmith, and even to prepare for moving homeward. An official synopsis of the papers,* then given to the press by the military authorities, does not fully establish the truth of the rumour, but it does give fair ground to infer that such an influence was exerted upon the counsels of Pretoria by the operations in Cape Colony; notably by the battle of Belmont, November 24, and the consequent demoralisation among the Free State burghers.

Whatever foundation of truth it may have, the incident irresistibly suggests, though it does not certainly demonstrate, the advantage of adhering to the original plan of advance by the Free State line. It has been stated that, "On all sides in Germany the opinion is expressed that Kimberley, and even Ladysmith, ought to have been erased as primary factors in the calculations of those responsible for the plan of operations. A strong British army advancing towards Bloemfontein, and turning neither to the left nor to the right, would have attracted the attention of all the

* Burleigh, "Natal Campaign," p. 129.

available Boer forces, and would indirectly, but none the less speedily, have relieved the pressure on Ladysmith and Kimberley. . . . War is a hard trade, and must be waged independently of minor considerations and of many human sympathies." * Would it not be juster to say, war must be waged in the spirit of fortitude, that endures the strain of even a very great risk, incurred by persisting in a course of action demonstrably correct?

Uttered in the week following Magersfontein and Colenso, the opinions just quoted are certainly open to the charge of being wise after the event; nevertheless, it is indisputable that they express a fundamental military truth. A really strong military conception would have been to concentrate for an advance, such as here suggested, notifying Sir George White that he could not expect direct relief, but must plan for a resistance protracted to the farthest, in order that upon the enemy might be thrown the dilemma of dividing his forces, thus facilitating the advance of the British central column, or else,

* London *Weekly Times*, December 22, 1899.

in order to oppose this, to drop the eagerly-coveted prize at Ladysmith. Divided as the total British force already was by the isolation of the latter, the great resolve would have been, "Let it fall, if it ultimately must, if only by endurance it prolongs to the latest moment the dissemination of the enemy's armies." One is forcibly reminded of the charge of the Archduke Charles to his subordinate at the critical moment of 1796, which Jomini singles out for conspicuous eulogium: "It matters not if Moreau gets to Vienna, provided you keep him occupied till I am done with Jourdan." Reasonings like these are strictly general in their bearing, liable to refutation by the special circumstances controlling a particular action; and it may perfectly well be that considerations of urgency, amounting even to impossibility, make them inapplicable to the case before us. Nevertheless, it can scarcely fail that, till such special considerations are known, and their validity admitted, it is to this point that military scrutiny and inquiry will be irresistibly drawn.

Whatever the cause of Joubert's retirement, the fact was beyond doubt on the evening of November 25, and on the 26th Hildyard had advanced a detachment twelve miles, to Frere, hoping thence to act upon the enemy's line of retreat. Herein he was disappointed, but with this began the general advance of the British forces in Natal, which a fortnight later brought the adversaries confronting one another on the opposite banks of the Tugela. During this period White also was not idle. Two well-planned and energetic night attacks were made upon the enemy's siege batteries — on the 8th of December at Gun Hill, a kopje pertaining to Lombard's Kop, and on the 10th at Surprise Hill, north of the town, towards Nicholson's Nek. The former, executed chiefly by Natal colonial forces, resulted in destroying a 6-inch gun and a 4·7-inch howitzer. The second, by Imperial troops, destroyed another howitzer of the same size. Like the sorties of Kekewich from Kimberley, these, by compelling the enemy's attention to the place, contributed to further the movements of Buller, between whom and the garrison communication, hitherto dependent chiefly upon runners, had now been opened by heliograph and electric-light signals.

Frere had now become the British point of assembly. On the 8th of December there were there concentrated four infantry brigades, designated numerically as the 2nd, 4th, 5th and 6th, as well as the cavalry and artillery, which a week later took part in the battle of Colenso. The Boers on their side had taken advantage of the interior position they held, between the relieving column and the garrison, and of the fact that the latter could scarcely attempt to break out to the north, to withdraw their forces in great measure from the latter quarter, disposing them between Ladysmith and the Tugela in such wise that they might most easily be concentrated upon the centre, should the British attack be made there, as it first was, or upon either flank should a turning manœuvre be attempted. Their arrangements for such action appear to have been sagaciously made, as were also the preparations for contesting the passage of the river at Colenso.

On December 12 the final British movement began by the advance to Chieveley of the 6th Brigade, styled also the Fusilier Brigade, under Major-General Barton, with 1,000 colonial cavalry, three field batteries—eighteen pieces—and a number of naval guns, of which two were of 4·7-inches calibre, and fourteen were long-range 12-pounders. These were drawn by oxen, even when going into action; the two heavier guns requiring each fourteen yoke. These batteries were manned by 254 seamen, under the command of Captain Jones, of the cruiser "Forte." The detachment thus composed settled down a little in advance of Chieveley, just east of the railroad line, about three miles from Colenso and four from the kopjes on the far side of the Tugela overlooking the railroad bridge, upon the nearest of which stands Fort Wylie. The exact range to the latter, as determined the next day, was 7,200 yards.*

The following morning, Wednesday, December 13, at 7 A.M., the naval guns began a heavy bombardment upon the kopjes last

* Four statute miles equal 7,040 yards

mentioned, which lie nearly due north of Colenso, and upon which Sir Redvers Buller intended to make his main attack. The firing was maintained for six hours, and did in places considerable damage to such works as could be discerned; the 4·7-inch guns using lyddite shells, the bursting effect of which is extremely violent. Despite the severity of the test to which they were thus subjected, the Boers with admirable self-control refrained from any reply, and so preserved in great part the secret of their dispositions from detection by the enemy.

Next day, Thursday the 14th, the remaining British force marched out of Frere camp at 4.30 A.M. for Chieveley. The extreme heat of the days, summer being then well begun, combine with the usual advantages of timely starting to determine early movements in South Africa. The last comers pitched camp west of the rail, and about a mile nearer the Tugela than the 6th Brigade. The naval guns also moved forward three-quarters of a mile, and resumed the bombardment. The Boers again making no reply, the disappointment of their opponents at failing to uncover the position of their guns began to yield to an impression that these had been withdrawn, and even that possibly the passage would not be contested.

The total British armament now gathered on the south side of the Tugela has been variously stated at from 20,000 to 23,000 of all arms. The smaller figure seems the more probable. As regards the number of their opponents, there is no certain information. Nothing is known, however, to reduce the estimate previously given—30,000. Allowing for the necessity of holding in check the garrison at Ladysmith, the Boers could very well meet Buller in force numerically equal, without taking account of the passive advantages of a defensive position unusually strong.

That night were distributed the British orders for forcing the passage of the Tugela. They were issued by Sir Francis Clery, as commanding the South Natal Field Forces; but Sir Redvers Buller, by the language of his subsequent report, has left no doubt that the plan embodied his own ideas, as Commander-in-Chief in South Africa generally, but present on this scene. This report is the guide in the following account, the narratives of others having been by the writer used to supplement or, where necessary, to elucidate.

The general line of the Tugela, for a half-dozen miles above Colenso, is nearly due east, but its course is extremely winding. In this section two or three bends of nearly a mile in bulge occur, one of which had quite an influence in the action. The town itself lies in a bight of this kind, just west of the railroad, which crosses the river by a bridge, at that time destroyed. Immediately above it, however, an iron road-bridge still remained. The latter is the centre of a semicircle of hills, which surround it to the northward, their crests being on an average some 1,400 feet high and distant four and a half miles. The bridge was also the centre of battle, as planned by the British. Near it, on the north side, are "four small, lozenge-shaped, steep-sided, hog-backed hills," the one nearest the water, on which Fort Wylie stands, being the lowest, the others rising in succession behind. They were all "strongly entrenched, with well-built, rough stone walls along every crest that offered, there being in some cases three tiers." It was upon these that Buller designed to make his principal effort. "It was a very awkward position to attack," he says, "but I thought that if I could effect a lodgment under cover of Fort Wylie the other hills would to a great extent mask each other, and shell-fire and want of water would clear them out in time."

The report of the Commander-in-Chief, dealing almost exclusively with the course of events as they happened, does not particularly describe the remaining features of the field. These must be supplied from other sources. Above—west of—Fort Wylie, on the north side, the hills recede somewhat from the river and rise to one of the crests mentioned by Buller, known as Grobler's Kloof. This also was heavily fortified, commanding, it is said, Fort Wylie and the neighbouring hills. If this be so, success at the latter, had it been achieved, would quickly have elicited proof of the fact. Under Grobler's Kloof, some two or three miles up the river, was a bridle-drift or ford, over which the plan of attack proposed to pass the 5th or Irish Brigade, commanded by Major-General Hart, forming the left flank of the British line. This done, the brigade would move down stream to reinforce the main attack on the Fort Wylie kopjes.

Below Fort Wylie the river continued south-easterly for something less than a mile. Then with a bold sweep it curves north, and round west, to a point half a mile north-east of the fort, when it again flows due north for a couple of miles. From this formation results a tongue of land, embraced in the curve, projecting to the south-east, and much resembling a bastion, to which the subsequent northern stretch serves as a curtain. In general effect, however, the river may be broadly said to make below Wylie a sharp turn to the north, running that way for two or three miles, after which it resumes its general easterly course towards the sea. The point where it thus resumes its direction is well to the north—rear—of the line of Boer entrenchments, between Grobler's and Wylie, so that, if their positions were prolonged on that same line, they would be separated by the river. If, on the other hand, instead of so continuing, the entrenched works were made to follow the river course north, keeping always on the same side of the Tugela, the main Boer positions, confronting the bridge, would be open to enfilading fire from the eastern hills on the opposite side below the bend.

Such conditions would seem to make this eastern part of the Boers' position—their left flank—the weakest. The outcome of the campaign tends to confirm this conclusion, which the author has been interested to find also in a letter, not only composed, but published, before the abortive attempt to turn the west flank at Spion Kop. "To the east of Fort Wylie," wrote a correspondent of the London *Times* on December 21, "the Tugela bends sharply northward, and here the left flank of the Boer position is on the south sides of the river, on a solitary hill called Hlangwane. This is doubtless the weakest spot in the Boer position, for if an enemy could take it by storm or otherwise, he could render the kopjes north of Colenso untenable." * This shows that the Boers preferred to have their lines divided by a river fordable only in places, and at times impassable through floods, rather than leave their flank uncovered to artillery, a decision probably correct. As shown by the plans, Hlangwane, as an eminence, stood by itself; a mile and a half to its east and rear was another height named Monte Christo, and again to the westward a range called Inhlawe Mountain.

Of the features mentioned, the Bridle Drift on the west, the iron road-bridge in the centre, and Hlangwane Hill on the east, are the principal points to remember. On the British side of the river, a plain sloped gradually down to the southern bank from a distance of two or three miles. It was divided north and south by a slight swell in the ground, flat-topped, of height just sufficient to conceal men on one side of it from

* London *Weekly Times*, January 19, 1900. On the other hand, another correspondent who shared this view has said, "The consensus of military opinion seems to be that the ground being too rough and broken to the eastward, the chief column will try and effect a crossing far to the westward of Colenso." (Burleigh—p. 155).

those on the other. On the eastern edge of this rise, the railroad track ran north to the bridge. On the western side, and between 3000 and 4000 yards from Wylie, was placed the chief naval battery, the two 4·7-inch and four 12-pounders. Between these and the railroad was to advance the central column of attack, the 2nd Brigade under General Hildyard. To the left rear of this, between it and the 5th Brigade—which, as before said, was directed upon the Bridle Drift—was placed the 4th, under Major General Lyttelton, charged with the duty of reinforcing either the 2nd or the 5th, as circumstances might demand during the progress of the fight. The 6th Brigade—Major-General Barton—was to advance on the east of the railroad, in general support of Hildyard. On this part of the field the ground was flat, but intersected by several dongas. Each extreme of the line of infantry formed by the four brigades was covered as usual by a flanking force, chiefly of horse; but while that on the British left had this function only, that on the right, the mounted brigade, with one battery—six guns

—was to attempt Hlangwane Hill. If successful, it was to enfilade the Wylie kopjes from that position. The remaining four batteries of field artillery were intended at the proper moment to concentrate their fire upon the Wylie kopjes, preparing the way for the crucial charge of the 2nd Brigade. For this object, two followed Lyttelton's 4th Brigade, and two the 6th; the last, under Colonel Long, being accompanied by six naval 12-pounders.

From these dispositions it appears, as is clearly stated by Buller in his report, that all the differing factors in the attack were to converge for their object, and according to their respective qualities, upon "the kopjes north of the iron bridge"—to use Clery's expression in the orders for battle. The 2nd Brigade marched upon them direct; the 5th approached their right flank by way of the Bridle Drift; the 4th and 6th reinforced, as required, each of the others; the four batteries—two on either side — brought a cross-fire upon the same objects; while the flanking force on the British right was to assist by an enfilading fire from Hlangwane. To combine several separate efforts, so that by mutual support and effect each at the critical moments contributes its due share to the one main exertion, is always difficult. Failure may ensue from lack of the nicest attention on the part of any one subordinate, or from those chances which must always be allowed for in war. The British at Colenso suffered from both causes.

Hart, on the left, having the longest road to reach the kopjes, moved first. The brigade reached the river, but missed the ford. It has been said that the enemy, by building a dam below, had raised the water to seven feet. Be that as it may, a few venturing in with musket and ammunition belts were drowned. Groping for the way, and apparently confused between the tortuous courses of the river itself and a tributary which enters near by, the mass of the troops blundered into a sharp bend curving to the northward, thus coming under a cross fire from the two enclosing banks. Here they became heavily engaged, and Buller, seeing the hopelessness of the position, recalled them. It was necessary, however, to send two of Lyttelton's battalions and two batteries to extricate them. Hart's attack therefore had failed, and his division contributed nothing further except the menace of its presence, which must retain some of the enemy to resist a possible renewal.

A yet more decisive mishap meanwhile had occurred in another part of the field. Reckoning that Hart and Hildyard were to attack in mutual support, the time had come for the latter to advance, and he had done so. The beginning of his movement was to have been covered by the six naval 12-pounders accompanying Long's two field batteries, and a position had been appointed them to that effect; it being intended apparently that the army guns should not come into action till later, when the development of Hildyard's movement would permit them to approach the enemy within their shorter range without losing the necessary support of infantry fire, —directly by the 6th brigade, specifically charged with that duty, and indirectly by the occupation which Hildyard's attack would necessarily give the Boers. Instead, however, of attending closely to the requirements of a movement where a certain exactness of touch was evidently necessary, Long's two field batteries, leaving their infantry escort behind, galloped rapidly forward on the east side of the railroad and came into action 1200 yards from Fort Wylie, and, as Buller judged, only 300* yards from the enemy's rifle pits. The slow-moving oxen fortunately were unable to drag the heavier naval guns to the same position to share the fate that quickly befell. A very heavy fire was opened from the Boer rifle pits, and although the gunners stuck manfully to their pieces until the ammunition in the limbers was exhausted, they were compelled then to leave them on the plain, retreating for shelter to a donga. The breech-blocks, even, were not carried away; it is said because they expected to return again to action. The naval detachment, 300 yards further back, were exposed to the same fire, but received only its outer fringe. The native drivers bolted, and many of the oxen were killed or stampeded; but

* This "3" in the copy before me may be a misprint for "8." The London *Times* correspondent gives 800 yards for the rifle fire.

the seamen contrived to drag their guns out of range.

News of this mishap reached Buller as he was returning from witnessing Hart's discomfiture. Hildyard was directed to move two regiments of his advancing brigade to the right to save the pieces; but, though the order was steadily executed, it was found impossible to keep the troops out of cover under the fire of Wylie, which had been momentarily silenced by Long's impetuous attack, but had now opened again. The batteries had failed by preceding, and so losing, infantry support; the infantry in turn failed because the guns were powerless. A sudden and desperate rush with harnessed teams succeeded in withdrawing two of the twelve abandoned pieces, in performing which service the son of Lord Roberts lost his life. But a second attempt found the enemy on guard again, and out of 22 horses that started 13 were killed before half-way to the spot.

The naval 12-pounder accompanying Long having been rendered immobile for the day, and the two batteries sacrificed, Sir Redvers Buller decided that without their support it would be impossible to force the passage. He therefore directed a general withdrawal to the camp. The abandoned batteries were left in the open, where, together with the wounded men and some of the supports sent in by Hildyard, they were taken by the Boers. The British loss in missing and prisoners was 21 officers and 207 men. There were killed 135, and wounded 762. The enemy remained unshaken in his positions.

This mortifying reverse, following sharply upon the heels of Magersfontein and Stormberg, thoroughly aroused the British people, who neither at home nor on the field were prepared for it. The day after the receipt of the news, Saturday, December 16th, a Cabinet meeting was held, and the next evening it was announced that, as the campaign in Natal was likely to require the undivided attention of Sir Redvers Buller, Lord Roberts would be sent to South Africa as Commander-in-Chief, and would be accompanied by Lord Kitchener as Chief of Staff. At the same time the rest of the Army Reserve was called out, and further measures taken which carried the troops employed in South Africa to, and beyond, the large numbers already quoted as despatched by the end of the following March.

Lord Roberts sailed from England December 23rd. On the 26th, at Gibraltar, he picked up Kitchener, who had been brought there by a swift naval cruiser, and on the 10th of January, 1900, he landed at Cape Town.

CHAPTER VI

THE NATAL CAMPAIGN. BRITISH PREPARE FOR A FLANKING ATTACK UPON THE BOERS' RIGHT AT THE TUGELA. THE BOER ASSAULT ON LADYSMITH, JANUARY 6TH.

AFTER the reverse at Colenso, nearly four weeks elapsed before Sir Redvers Buller was ready to move again for the relief of Ladysmith. The interval passed in receiving reinforcements, and in accumulating a transport service which should enable the army to perform a long flanking march, for, the frontal attack upon the Boer centre having failed, and its difficulties been not only recognised but demonstrated, the purpose was now to turn their right flank by way of Springfield, some twenty miles to the north-east of Frere, crossing thence the Tugela by a ford six miles distant, known as Trichardt's Drift, and following the Acton Homes road.

The army would thus pass round Spion Kop and gain the open plain north of the mountain thus named.

While this movement was in progress, but before crossing the river, a reserve supply for seventeen days was accumulated at Springfield. It may be assumed therefore that this represents the conditions which Sir Redvers Buller thought requisite to his projected operation. The necessity of depending chiefly upon the slow-moving ox-wagons, and their comparatively small capacity, made the organising of the train tedious and difficult. "To forward supply alone," vrote Buller, "took 650 ox-wagons, and as between Frere and Springfield there are three places where all the wagons had to be double-spanned, and some required three spans, some idea of the difficulties may be formed." A correspondent with the army states that the wagons "can only be depended upon to haul not more than 600 pounds each." To lessen this great inconvenience road traction-engines were employed with success. The same writer says of these that "they can easily haul twelve tons, and on a flat, dry veldt strip along at a brisk eight miles an hour. They leisurely descend into spruits—beds of streams—roll across, and wheel up stiff long climbs like flies walking up a wall. They are not quite helpless, even when the ground has been soaked by rain." *

While these preparations were making, the besieged had to resign themselves to further weary endurance. "Sir Redvers Buller," writes a correspondent within, "has sent a heliograph message bidding us wait in patience for another month until siege artillery can reach him." The bombardment was maintained by the Boers with increased but monotonous regularity, intensified from time to time as movements among Buller's troops led them to strengthen their forces upon the Tugela, with a consequent weakening of those of investment.

The firm resolve manifested by the British Government and people after the repulse at Colenso, and the enlargement at once given to the scale of the war and to the contemplated reinforcements, showed that,

* Burleigh, "Natal Campaign," p. 240.

unless the garrison was speedily reduced, it would probably be relieved by sheer weight of numbers. In short, the opportunity for a decisive blow possibly now existed, but, if not quickly improved, would certainly pass away for ever. The motive for the assault that soon followed is not positively known; but, if the Boer information of the damage done by their shells, and of the food and ammunition supply in the town, was as accurate as it is believed to have been, they knew that neither bombardment nor hunger could reduce the place before the dreaded power of the outside enemy received full development. Ladysmith was to them like a dead weight round the neck of a swimmer struggling for life under other disadvantages. It is unnecessary to seek any further reason for the assault of January 6, by whomsoever first commanded. The words attributed to Joubert's order, "Ladysmith must be taken before Wednesday"—the faint echo, perhaps, of Wellington's "Ciudad Rodrigo *must* be stormed this evening"—needed only to be supplemented by the words, "or never," to express a military argument to which no valid reply could be made. As the commander of the New Orleans forts said, "There will be no to-morrow unless so and so is done *at once.*"

Reluctant, therefore, though the Boers as a race have shown themselves to offensive tactics and to assault, the necessities of the case compelled them. In their plan, and in its execution, they showed all the courage, all the tenacity, heretofore displayed in their defensive operations, as well as the peculiar, stealthy rockcraft of a nation of hunters, which has equally characterised them. It is not, however, too much to add that at the supreme moment, when man stands foot to foot and eye to eye, and when the issue depends upon superior aggressive momentum of temperament, the national trait, whether original or acquired, asserted itself; and the heroes who had scaled the heights barefoot, and clung with undying resolution to their rocky cover, exchanging shots almost muzzle to muzzle, did not muster the resolution which might, or might not—the true soldier recks not which at such an hour—have carried them, more than decimated, but triumphant, across the belt of withering fire to victory. The reply of the British colonel on the other side of the sixty yards of plateau that separated the opponents, "We will try"—a phrase which Americans will remember fell in the same tongue from the lips of our own Colonel Miller at Lundy's Lane—expressed just the difference. Of the three companies who then rose to their feet on Wagon Hill and rushed, every officer fell and fifty-five of the men; but the bayonets of the survivors reached the other side, and there followed the inevitable result. The men that would not charge fled.

Of this affair, in which Ladysmith most nearly touched ruin, the salient details only must be briefly told. The part of the British defences chosen for the Boer assault was a ridge two miles south of the town, in length some 4,500 yards,—over two and a half miles,—and 600 feet high. Its general direction is east and west, but in contour it is slightly concave towards the south, whence the assailants came. In the centre, this crescent, having a comparatively easy incline, is more readily swept by fire, and approach is more easily seen. The Boers consequently chose to ascend by the horns, which are very precipitoùs, and where, therefore, if no noise is made, detection is not easy and aim is extremely difficult. Above the ridge thus described rose three eminences, of 100 feet or more. That on the east was Cæsar's Camp, about 1,500 yards long by 700 wide; next, and 400 yards distant, Wagon Hill, two-thirds the size; and close to this, and at the extreme west, Wagon Hill West, scarcely more than a knob, but very steep.

The Boer plan was to seize the two extremities by a night attack of picked men, who, when they had made good their hold, would be reinforced rapidly from a main body assembled behind hills some two miles south. Against Wagon Hill went 300 men, who, on reaching the foot, took off their shoes and divided into two parties, one of which climbed noiselessly Wagon Hill, the other Wagon Hill West. They came as a complete surprise upon the British outposts. Wagon Hill West was held by two squadrons, about 70 men, of Natal troopers—the Imperial Light Horse; Wagon Hill proper by a half-battalion of infantry. It happened, however, by fortunate coincidence, that it had been decided to mount that night a naval gun upon Wagon Hill West. This, with an escort of engineer troops, a half company of infantry, and some seamen—in all sixty rifles—had reached the foot of the hill by 2.30 A.M., the hour the attack was made.

Alarm was taken only an instant before the Boers were upon the garrison. The rush and fire followed so instantly that the defenders were driven in disorder over the crest, leaving it in the hands of the enemy, who captured a lieutenant and sixteen men—thirteen of them wounded. Amid the surprise and confusion, and the black darkness, the gun escort, under two young lieutenants of engineers, held firm, affording a rallying point for the routed garrison ; and this mixed body, steadying itself under cover on the reverse side of the hill, stood fast and waited events. The Boers, also expectant, instead of pursuing their success, retired and sought cover on the outer slope ; a narrow sixty yards of summit alone separating the opponents.

Somewhat less of success attended the surprise on Wagon Hill proper. Nevertheless, there also the Boers effected a lodgment on the plateau, and along the nek connecting with Wagon Hill West. A group of stragglers, from the Imperial Light Horse and the Wagon Hill garrison, had got together among the boulders of a knoll off the latter hill, near the nek, and thence kept up a cross-fire on Wagon Hill West. The Boers doing the same from their side, that summit was untenable to either party. Here, at the west end of Wagon Hill, the two lines were but 30 yards apart. To the eastward, towards Cæsar's Camp, as the plateau widened, the space increased to 100 yards. The danger to the British in this situation was, that if the knoll were lost, Wagon Hill West, losing the support of its fire, would probably fall with it. Wagon Hill proper would then be taken in flank as well as in front, and so rendered untenable; while Wagon Hill once gone, Cæsar's Camp would be exposed to a like concentration and probably to the same fate. Deprived of the ridge, the British line of defences would be broken and the enemy established on a commanding height in easy range—5,000 yards—of the town. Two or three desperate attempts to reinforce the knoll by crossing the open were therefore made by small parties, but these were cut down, the officers leading them being killed. At this time the colonel, two majors, and four other officers of the Light Horse were hit. It was to this resolute tenure of the key of the situation by a handful of men that Sir George White referred in a speech at Belfast. "On January 6th, which has been alluded to as a tight day, had it not been for the Imperial Light Horse, Joubert might have been spending his Sunday (January 7) where I spent mine. I think I may say of them they were the bravest men I ever had under my command." Colonel Ian Hamilton, the brigadier in command on the ridge, also wrote of them, "It will be made quite clear in my despatch that the Imperial Light Horse were second to none. No one realizes more clearly than I do that they were the backbone of the defence during that long day's fighting."* In other parts of the field also the British loss of officers at this moment was heavy.

At dawn the lines lay as described, but

* Burleigh's "Natal Campaign," p. 410.

reinforcements were being hurried to the British, the greater part directed on Cæsar's Camp. The Boers did not move during this critical period, relying upon their deadly fire, maintained by veterans in cover-taking and marksmanship. More than this was needed. In such a state of the national cause, the crests should have been attempted at all risks; and at all risks the forlorn hopes should have received immediate substantial support. In cases like this, national temperament tells; there was by them no such rush as those in which the British officers had dared to fail. By 8 A.M., more or less, Wagon Hill and Wagon Hill West had received, or saw coming, reinforcements of a half battalion of infantry and two fresh squadrons of the Imperial Light Horse. The Boers, however, were also pushing men up. Under these conditions no further advance was tried from either line, but the firing continued incessant and unpitying. By 10 A.M. the British force had so increased that the Boer fire was considerably slackened.

While these things were happening on the west, Cæsar's Camp had been also the scene of a contest—serious, and for a moment apparently doubtful. At no time, however, was the peril here as great as on Wagon Hill. There the fight was lost, and there won. Meantime the Boer siege guns had opened upon the field of action with great effect, maintaining a vigorous fire throughout; and the British on their side had advanced field batteries in the plain, to sweep either flank of the threatened ridge, a measure which markedly curtailed the power of the enemy to send reinforcements to those already engaged on the heights. The Boers had also developed attacks upon the north and north-east of the town; but these, however intended, did not proceed beyond mere demonstrations.

At 2 P.M., on Wagon Hill West, a few Boers at last attempted what numbers should have tried hours before. It is trite to say that at such a crisis proverbial truths receive double emphasis. "Not to gain ground is to lose ground." "He who hesitates is lost." At the hour named, a number—eight, it is said—at their head De Villiers, a Free State commander, rose suddenly to their feet. The action, unexpected after so many passive hours, shook the steadiness of the British opposite. Some turned and ran down hill, but the Engineer detachment stood fast with fixed bayonets. An infantry major beside them fell, shot dead, but their own lieutenant, Digby Jones, a youth in his twenties, led them forward to the encounter. The parties met midway, but only one follower had kept on with Villiers. The Boer leader was killed by Jones, who himself dropped immediately after. His junior, Denniss, went out to look for him, and quickly shared his fate. So, after hours of steadfast bearing, died these gallant lads—not in vain. With them fell also fifteen out of their thirty sappers, wounded, but not all slain.

At 4 P.M. a rain-storm of exceptional violence, even for South Africa, burst over the ridge. In the midst of it the Boers on Wagon Hill West, whose numbers had increased beyond the British knowledge, again attempted a forward movement; again, so the accounts say, waverers were found on the British side; again their officers called them together; charge threatened was met with charge effected, and for the last time.

Before the levelled bayonets the enemy turned and fled down hill to return no more.

The same opportunity of tempest was taken by the assailants on Wagon Hill to mass their forces. Then it was that the British commander on the spot asked Colonel Park whether, with the three companies of the Devonshire Regiment in reserve, he could clear the hill. "We will try," was the reply. The companies deployed in three lines, in extended order—six to eight paces between the men—and fixed bayonets. The enemy knew not what was coming, but their watch was untiring. When ready, "The Colonel rose to his feet, and the three companies rose with him as one man. With a cheer that foretold success, the Devons dashed into the open. The fire with which they were received was simply awful; it might have staggered any troops. Leaving the cover of the stones, the Boers stood upright and emptied their magazines into the advancing line. But it never wavered, never checked, though the ranks were sadly thinned. The Boers fled from the boulders which they had held with such tenacity throughout the day, and turned at bay upon the edge of the crest, hoping yet to stay the deadly rush of steel. They were augmented from below, but the stand was of no avail. Though charging, the Devons steadily changed front and bore down upon the hillside. The enemy broke and fled headlong down. The day was won. Such was their dread of the bayonet, they did not even attempt to rally in the spruits below, but, leaving prisoners and ammunition behind, without turning, made their way to their horses." * A bayonet charge rarely is awaited.

Ladysmith was saved, but at heavy cost. The British loss in killed was—officers, 14; private men, 164; wounded officers, 33; privates, 287; of the latter, 4 officers and 25 men died of their wounds. The Boers' loss is not accurately known. A correspondent in Ladysmith has stated that Sir George White, having undertaken to deliver the bodies of those who fell within the British lines, 133 were so handed over from the top of the

* London *Weekly Times*, February 23, 1900. In default of official reports, the author has depended chiefly upon the *Times* correspondence, and upon "Four Months Besieged," by Mr. H. H. Pearse, correspondent of the *Daily News*.

hill. This number was believed to be small compared to those slain on the retreat, on the slopes, and in the brush below. The streams being in flood from the rain, it was thought that many more were drowned. In estimating hostile losses, however, there is usually a tendency to exaggerate.

The Boers never again attempted assault.

CHAPTER VII

NATAL CAMPAIGN. THE UNSUCCESSFUL BRITISH ATTEMPTS TO TURN THE BOERS' RIGHT FLANK AT SPION KOP AND AT VAAL KRANTZ

ON the 9th of January, 1900, the Fifth Division of the British Army, which, under Lieut.-General Sir Charles Warren, had been assembling at Estcourt, marched out for Frere, where General Buller's headquarters had been established after the battle of Colenso. Arriving the same evening, it started the next day for Springfield, the movement being followed by the whole army, except the 6th Brigade, left at Chieveley, and such other troops as were needed to protect the railroad to Durban against raids. To control the action of the mass of the Boers, dependence could be placed upon the operation in progress for turning their right flank, to resist which and to maintain the siege of Ladysmith would require all the force at their disposal.

The abortive issue of this British undertaking, and of its sequent operation against Vaal Krantz in the same quarter, removes the necessity of giving minute details in a narrative which does not profess to be a critical military study, but merely seeks to present a clear analytical account of the various transactions.

It is necessary first to understand the principal features of the country. In general directions, as far as effective, the movement followed the valley of the Tugela. In this, ten miles west of Colenso, there is a sharp bend at nearly right angles. There the stream for a stretch of six miles has run south by east, while above it the river bed again, as below, lies east and west, but is excessively tortuous, winding back and forth among hills which on one side or the other come down close to the water's edge. It was at Trichardt's Drift, about seven miles above—west of—this north and south stretch, that the British army was to make, and did make, its crossing; purposing thereby to turn the flanks of the Boer positions, which in a general sense followed the north bank of the Tugela.

The conditions leading to the choice of this point appear to have been as follows. Eastward of the north and south stretch just specified, and as far as to the Ladysmith railroad, the mountain ranges north of the river are not only high, but wide, broken, and intricate, ending in Grobler's Kloof and the other kopjes mentioned in describing the positions at Colenso. The reverse slopes of this broken region are full six miles north of the river's course. The map shows the district almost wholly bare of roads, an indication that it is unsuited to large military operations. Upstream of the stretch, the ranges, though steep and broken, are very much narrower. Three miles west of it, at Potgieter's Drift, a road passes through from Springfield to the plain beyond at Brakfontein, showing a considerable depression at this point. By this road was made the second unsuccessful attempt of the campaign, towards Vaal Krantz.

Four miles higher up, at Trichardt's Drift

the chain leaves the river, trending north-north-west for eight miles, with a breadth which, beginning with three miles at the south, narrows to one and a half, with lessening elevation, towards the north end, where it drops to the plain. The western slope of this eight mile spur, over the southern part of which, contrary to first intention, the British attack was actually made, is precipitous near the summit; lower down it is more gradual, but still steep. A mile from the foot of the spur, and parallel to it, runs a stream called Venter's Spruit, which enters the Tugela from the north-west a little above Trichardt's. Six miles from the ford, between spur and spruit, is Acton Homes, the point designated by Buller as the first objective of the army, whence the range was to be crossed. The change of direction noted at Trichardt's gives to the whole range, from Colenso to Acton Homes, the character of an arc of a circle, on the interior of which, considered as a defensive position, the Boers moved, with the additional advantage of being all mounted men. Near the southern end of the spur, but well to its eastern edge, is the lofty eminence called Spion Kop, which played so important a part in the operation as it ultimately developed.

At Acton Homes roads meet from north, south, east and west; a fact which sufficiently indicates the importance of the point and the comparatively favourable nature of the surroundings for operations — for roads usually seek the easiest ground. From it two start east for Ladysmith, crossing the spur by different ways, and uniting some eight miles beyond in the plain lying west of Ladysmith, where the network of communications shows the relatively open character of the country. It was by one or both of these roads that Buller purposed to advance.

On the 12th of January the 5th Division reached Springfield, and on the 13th the whole army was assembled there or at Spearman's Hill, near Potgieter's Drift, where Buller established his headquarters. The hills there on the south side of the river were fortunately secured, and naval batteries placed upon them commanding the opposite heights. The turning movement by way of Acton Homes was then committed by Sir Redvers

Buller to Sir Charles Warren, who on the 15th of January received—to quote his own words — "secret instructions to command a force to proceed across the Tugela, near Trichardt's Drift, to the west of Spion Kop, recommending me to proceed forward, refusing my right (Spion Kop), and bringing my left forward to gain the open plain north of Spion Kop . . . I was provided with four days' rations, with which I was to cross the Tugela, fight my way round to north of Spion Kop, and join your column opposite Potgieter's." This, therefore, was Buller's plan; the spur was to be turned rather than forced. It appears to have been his sustained purpose to leave the execution to Warren, interfering himself not at all or the very least possible. The force employed on the expedition has been nowhere found officially stated. Warren himself says that his own command "amounted to an army corps less one brigade," which, including all arms and the medical and supply services, would be about 30,000 men—an estimate that appears rather too high. The one brigade remained with Buller at Spearman's Camp.

On the evening of January 16 this brigade, the 4th, under Lyttelton, covered by the naval batteries, crossed at Potgieter's Drift, and established itself in kopjes a mile north of the river. The movement was a feint on the Brakfontein Road, and was continued the following days to draw attention from the true attack by Warren. The latter crossed on the 17th at Trichardt's, occupied the hills on the north side commanding the ford, and pushed the cavalry as far as Acton Homes, which they entered without serious opposition, but were soon after withdrawn. That night and the 18th the wagon train passed over, and on the 19th two brigades advanced farther and occupied some hills on the right.

During the 19th Warren made up his mind that the plan "recommended" him was not practicable without modification, and, after consulting his principal subordinates, telegraphed that evening to Buller as follows: "I find there are only two roads north of the Tugela by which we could possibly get from Trichardt's Drift to Potgieter's—one by Acton Homes, the other by Fair View and Rosalie. The first I reject as too long; the second is a very difficult road for a large number of wagons unless the enemy is thoroughly cleared out. I am, therefore, going to adopt some special arrangement which will involve my stay at Venter's Laager for two or three days. I will send in for further supplies and report progress." Explained by other remarks of Warren's in his despatches, this appears to mean that the easier road by Acton Homes was thought by him too long for his division to traverse with the food they could carry in their haversacks, and that it was therefore necessary to take the shorter, which leaves the main road three miles from Trichardt's, and strikes directly over the range, passing north, and within three miles, of Spion Kop. To do this the men would carry four days' rations, and the wagons be returned south of the Tugela. First of all, however, the positions in front must be captured, including Spion Kop.

The above telegram was the only report made at this period by Warren to his superior. Various operations went on during the next three days, presumably pursuant of the purpose stated in Warren's subsequent account of his proceedings—"We must first capture the position in front of us." The estimate of their effect by Buller, who was at the scene on the 21st and 22nd, is best given in the words of his report to Lord Roberts. "I went over to Sir C. Warren on the 23rd. I pointed out to him that I had no further report and no intimation of the special arrangements foreshadowed by his telegram of the 19th, that for four days he had kept his men exposed to shell and rifle fire, perched on the edge of an almost precipitous hill, that the position admitted of no second line, and the supports were massed close behind the firing line in indefensible formations, and that a panic or sudden charge might send the whole lot in disorder down the hill at any moment. I said it was too dangerous a situation to be prolonged, and that he must either attack or I should withdraw his force. I advocated, as I had previously done, an advance from his left." This last phrase does not make certain whether Buller's judgment coincided with that of Warren concerning the impracticability of the Acton Homes route, but it seems to indicate that it did not.

Warren replied that he had intended to assault Spion Kop the night before, but had not done so because the general told off for the work wished first to reconnoitre the ground. It was decided that the attack should be made that night, and General Woodgate was detailed for the command at Buller's "suggestion"—or, to use Warren's words, "the Commander-in-Chief desired."

The assault was made that night and was entirely successful, the British gaining possession of the summit and remaining there all next day. It was found, however, that the Boers had guns in position on neighbouring heights within effective range. It was possible also for the Boer riflemen, with their extraordinary aptitudes for stalking, to maintain a perpetual fire from well-covered positions; whereas, to whatever cause attributable, there does not seem to have been a well-organised plan to provide artificially and rapidly the shelter which the flat bare tops of South African mountains do not naturally extend. General Woodgate was mortally wounded at 10 A.M. Reinforcements were then on the way, and when his fall was reported, General Coke, with two fresh regiments, was sent to assume command. He heliographed down at 2 P.M. that unless the enemy's guns could be silenced the men could not hold the place under another day's shelling. Some hours later, at 9.30 P.M., he was called down to make a personal report of the conditions.

Towards nightfall Warren made arrangements to send up two naval 12-pounders, a mountain battery, and a heavy working party under engineer direction to organise field protection—a provision that should have formed part of the original plan—elaborated through four days of operations. Before these reached the summit, and in ignorance that they were on the way, Colonel Thorneycroft, left in command by Coke's departure, decided that the position was untenable, and soon after 9.30 P.M. evacuated it. Upon this Sir Redvers Buller commented: "Preparations for the second day's defence should have been organised during the day, and have been commenced at nightfall. As this was not done I think Colonel Thorneycroft exercised a wise discretion." From this judgment Lord

Roberts dissented vigorously. "I am of opinion that Lieut.-Colonel Thorneycroft's assumption of responsibility and authority was wholly inexcusable. During the night the enemy's fire could not have been formidable, and . . . it would not have taken more than two or three hours at most to communicate by messenger with General Coke or Sir C. Warren, and to receive a reply. General Coke appears to have left Spion Kop at 9.30 P.M. for the purpose of consulting with Sir Charles Warren, and up to that hour the idea of a withdrawal had not been entertained. Yet, almost immediately after General Coke's departure Colonel Thorneycroft issued an order, without reference to superior authority, which upset the whole plan of operations, and rendered unavailing the sacrifices which had already been made to carry it into effect." In face of this severe, and in the author's judgment merited, condemnation, it would be less than just not to quote also Lord Roberts' further words. "Lieut.-Colonel Thorneycroft appears to have behaved in a very gallant manner throughout the day, and it was doubtless due in great measure to his exertions and example that the troops continued to hold the summit until directed to retire."

On the morning of the 25th, seeing that Spion Kop was no longer held, Buller assumed command in person, and began to withdraw to the south of the Tugela. This movement was completed on the 27th, the troops reaching their new camps by 10 A.M. of that day.

Thus, unfortunately, ended in failure an expedition concerning which Lord Roberts wrote, "The attempt was well devised, and I agree with Sir Redvers Buller in thinking that it ought to have succeeded." He continues, "That it failed may, in some measure, be due to the difficulties of the ground, and the commanding positions held by the enemy, probably also to errors of judgment and want of administrative capacity on the part of Sir Charles Warren. But, whatever faults Sir Charles Warren may have committed, the failure must also be ascribed to the disinclination of the officer in supreme command to assert his authority and see that what he thought best was done, and also to the unwarrantable and needless assumption of responsibility by a subordinate officer."

It would be presumptuous and unbecoming in an officer not of the land service to express an opinion upon the difficulties of detail encountered in the various operations of this week's work. But the points selected for criticism in the expressions of Lord Roberts just quoted belong to the fundamentals, common to both military professions. The generous wish of Sir Redvers Buller to leave his subordinate untrammelled discretion in the management of an operation intrusted to him, was pushed to an extreme, and was maintained, as is plainly evidenced by his own dispatch, after confidence was shaken. The situation was one familiar, on a smaller scale, to every officer who has ever had command. It is difficult at times to draw the line between fussy interference and reasonable superintendence; yet more difficult to determine the moment when a subordinate must be subjected to the mortification of virtual supersession in the control of a matter that has been committed to him. But these are, after all, only instances of embarrassments common to life, which increase in degree and in number as one mounts the ladder. Whatever may be said in favour of the fullest discretion to a subordinate out of signal distance—and very much indeed must be said for this—nothing can relieve a commander-in-chief only four miles distant of the responsibility, not for his own reputation—a small matter—but for his country's interests, in directing according to his own judgment the great operations of a campaign. However honourable to generosity, it is certainly carrying self-abnegation to an indefensible extreme to leave the decision of attack or withdrawal, of movement by direct attack or by flanking—"by the left"—to a junior, when one's self is on the spot, in actual conversation.

The action of Colonel Thorneycroft in withdrawing raises also the mooted question of when and how the assumption of responsibility in disobeying orders — express or implied, general or particular — is to be justified; a matter on which much unenlightened nonsense has lately been spoken and written in the United States. No general rule, indeed, can be laid down, but this much may surely be re-affirmed—that the justification of so serious a step must ever rest, not on the officer's *opinion* that he was doing right, but upon the fact, demonstrated to military judgment by the existing conditions, that he *was* right. Colonel Thorneycroft's intentions were doubtless of the best; the writer cannot but believe that Lord Roberts's sentence will be endorsed by the professions, for the reasons he himself gives.

After the withdrawal across Trichardt's Drift, a week was allowed for repose after the seven days' fighting just undergone. The attempt to reach Ladysmith was then renewed, taking the road by Potgieter's Drift to Brakfontein. It was decided first to get possession of Vaal Krantz, a height three or four miles east of Spion Kop, to the right of the road. The movement began on February 5th, under the immediate direction of Sir Redvers Buller. The same day Vaal Krantz was carried and occupied; but Buller was disappointed in the advantage he hoped from it. He reported that "it was necessary after seizing Vaal Krantz to entrench it as the pivot of further operations, but I found after trying for two days that, owing to the nature of the ground, this was not practicable; it was also exposed to fire from heavy guns which fired from positions by which our artillery was dominated."

As the projected advance depended upon the tenure of Vaal Krantz, and this could not be assured under the circumstances, the attempt had to be abandoned. On the evening of February 7 the British army again retired south of the Tugela, and thence returned to the camps at Chieveley, facing Colenso.

In the operations about Spion Kop from January 17–24, the British losses were: killed, officers 27, men 245; wounded, officers 53, men 1,050; missing and prisoners, officers 7, men 351. Total, 87 officers, 1646 men.

At Vaal Krantz, February 5–7, the losses were: killed, officers 2, men 23; wounded, officers 18, men 326; missing, men 5. Total, 20 officers, 354 men.

CHAPTER VIII

THE RELIEF OF KIMBERLEY AND OF LADYSMITH, AND THE SURRENDER OF CRONJE

THE month of February, 1900, which opened with the reverse at Vaal Krantz, proved to be the culminating period of the war. During its course, the tide, which had been running strongly against the British, turned decisively in their favour. Before it closed, Kimberley and Ladysmith had been relieved and Cronje forced to surrender.

After the affair at Magersfontein, December 11, Methuen and Cronje remained confronting one another. The British strengthened themselves upon the line of the Modder, by the railroad; the Boers, from the kopjes of Spytfontein, some three miles to the northward, gradually extended their works east and west until in both directions their flanks rested upon the river. Shelling by guns of long range was carried on intermittingly by both parties, and there were small affairs from time to time, but nothing on a large scale occurred.

After his arrival on January 10, Lord Roberts spent three weeks in Cape Town arranging for his campaign. On the 6th of February he left, accompanied by Lord Kitchener, and on the 9th was at the Modder Camp. On the 11th began the movement which resulted four days later in the relief of Kimberley, and on the 27th of the month in the surrender of Cronje. For these objects, and at this time, 44,000 troops of all arms had been collected near the Modder.

It is needless to say that preparation had preceded execution by more than the two or three days elapsing between Roberts' arrival and the start. At Cape Town he had had interviews with General French, summoned there for that purpose. During January the constant arrival of troops from all quarters at the Modder Camp gave the impression of a purpose to resume the frontal attack and to force the way to Kimberley through Magersfontein; an impression which, produced on the mind of the Boer leader, was itself part of the necessary preparation. On the 3rd of February, General Hector MacDonald, with a brigade of Highlanders, had moved north-west, towards Koodoosberg, where he arrived on the 7th. The movement was in sufficient force to attract the attention of the Boers, and appeared the more plausible because of the disturbed condition of the district; which, although British, was full of Boer partisans showing signs of restlessness. A similar expedition, but less numerous, under Colonel Pilcher, had gone out early in January, capturing forty rebels. While otherwise useful, it seems probably that MacDonald's enterprise was intended chiefly to fasten the enemy's attention in a false direction. On the 8th he was recalled by Methuen, acting under orders from headquarters.

The great projected operation was to turn the eastern left flank of Cronje's position, seizing important drifts, or fords, on the

Riet and Modder Rivers by a secret and rapid circuit of cavalry, which should hold them until they were secured by slower moving infantry following on the track. When the last and chief of these, Klip Drift on the Modder, some twenty miles east of Magersfontein, was held by an infantry division, the cavalry's flank would be secured and its advance would then be pressed to Kimberley. While the movement was in progress, Methuen in his old lines on the Modder would hold the enemy in his positions by a demonstration of force seemingly not reduced. If the undertaking were successful, superior British numbers would be planted across the line of Cronje's communications with Bloemfontein, and the cavalry on his rear to intercept retreat in mass to the north. To this turning operation were assigned three divisions of infantry and one of cavalry; the latter was under General French, called from the Naauwport district for this purpose. The infantry divisions were the 6th, General Kelly-Kenny; the 7th, General Tucker; and the 9th, General Colvile. The total force thus engaged in the invasion of the Orange

Free State was 34,000; 23,000 infantry and 11,000 mounted men. They were accompanied by 98 pieces of artillery, and by supplies in 700 wagons, drawn by 9,000 mules and oxen.

French's division, three brigades, 4,800 men, accompanied by seven batteries of horse artillery, left Modder River Camp at 3 A.M. Sunday, February 11th. Diverging slightly from the railroad, they marched due south—away from the enemy—seventeen miles to Ramdam, which is about ten miles east of Graspan Station. At sunrise they were out of sight of the empty tents, standing deceitfully behind them. At noon Ramdam was reached, and the division halted till 3 A.M. of the 12th, when it again marched due east for a ford called Waterval Drift, on the Riet River, which it will be remembered is a tributary of the Modder, flowing from south-east to north-west. Reaching there soon after sunrise, the ford was found to be held by a party of the enemy. Covering his change of purpose by a feint upon this position, French swung the rest of his division to the right, and with slight loss forced a passage at De Kiel's Drift, apparently somewhat higher up. That evening he held both sides of the Riet, the enemy having retreated. During the night Kitchener came up with a division of infantry which had made its journey in part by rail, and with which arrived also supply trains, whose slow movement would have delayed unduly the progress of the horse division.

Owing to delays in distributing provisions and fodder, French could not start again until 11.30 A.M. The loss of the five early hours, says an eye-witness, cost 100 horses, which died or failed in the march that day. The goal now was Klip Drift, about twenty-five miles distant. Passing well east of Jacobsdal, suffering intensely from heat and thirst, the division sighted the Modder when still eight miles away. All were much spent, the artillery horses could scarcely drag their pieces, and there was a showing of opposition on the right front; but French, despite the general exhaustion, decided to drive on without halting, lest the enemy, recovering from their surprise, should concentrate to oppose his passage. Thus hastening, the Boers, taken unready, were routed. At 5.35 P.M. French reported back to Roberts, who received the message at De Kiel's Drift, that he had occupied the hills on the north of the river, capturing three of the enemy's laagers with supplies, while Gordon with his brigade had seized Rondeval Drift, four miles west, with a second drift between it and Klip, and two more laagers. Control of both sides of the Modder, and power to operate on either bank freely, were thus assured, provided the infantry followed in time.

That night, February 13–14, the cavalry rested on the north bank, holding the adjacent kopjes, and there remained during the succeeding day, waiting for the infantry. Throughout the 14th the Boers made constant harassing demonstrations, disturbing the rest of the weary men and horses. "But no attack was driven home. 'Could the Boers learn to attack, they would be a formidable foe,' the General once observed. Directly we moved out the attack failed." * Kitchener in person arrived at midnight, and the 6th Division, "very tired," at early morning of the 15th.

* "The Cavalry Rush to Kimberley," by Captain Cecil Boyle, additional aide to General French. The *Nineteenth Century*, June, 1900, p. 907.

The defence of the position was then turned over to Kelly-Kenny, "leaving French free to act," * and the cavalry, reinforced by several new regiments from the westward, which raised its numbers to near 10,000,† prepared for the final rush to Kimberley, some twenty-five miles away.

A few miles from Klip Drift, towards Kimberley, lay an enclosed plain, five miles long by three wide, where a number of Boers were waiting to contest progress. The kopjes controlling entrance had been secured by the British, but the transit had to be forced. The enemy were in position on hills in front, and flanking the lines of advance. Measures were taken to cover the flanks with artillery, and to clear them while pressing forward, otherwise the Boer positions were carried by a charge. "The whole division was set in motion. For nearly five miles in perfect order they galloped on, until the head of the plain was reached. It was a thrilling time, never to be forgotten. Our guns held the enemy on our left, while the 9th and 16th Lancers had cleared the ground

* Lord Roberts' telegram.

† London *Weekly Times*, March 23, 1900, p. ii.; also February 23, p. 114.

on the right. About two miles from the head of the plain the main body was halted to allow the guns from the left to rejoin us, but Broadwood's brigade continued the gallop to the very top of the pass on the left, and the 12th Lancers dismounted and held the kopjes in front. The right front was held by the Household Composite and Gordon's Lancers." *

After a brief stop to re-assemble the march was resumed. Just beyond the head of the plain the chimneys of the mine works at Kimberley became visible—still ten miles distant. Cronje, by this aware of the direction and purpose of the movement, tried to intercept the advance at a place called Benaauwheidfontein Farm, four miles from the town, but he was just too late to occupy the commanding positions. Brushing aside the inadequate force opposing him, French passed on, and about 7 P.M. entered the place, joining hands with the long besieged. Kimberley was relieved, and the British cavalry established on Cronje's rear.

The general situation that evening, Thurs-

* "The Cavalry Rush to Kimberley," p. 909.

day, February 15, was as follows: Methuen at Magersfontein, in front of Cronje; the 7th Infantry Division at Jacobsdal, ten miles to the south-east; the 6th holding the Klip and Rondeval Drifts on the Modder, twenty miles east of the Boer army; the 9th near Jacobsdal, in reserve, ready to move where most needed. Lord Roberts himself was at Jacobsdal, whence his telegrams were dated on the 16th and 17th. Kitchener remained at Klip Drift.

Cronje, who had not believed that the British could make so rapid a march, or take so large a force far from the railroad, saw that not only had he been outwitted and his position become untenable, but that there was no time to lose if he hoped to escape at all. As French slipped by him into Kimberley, he sent word to the camp to get the trains at once in movement, and to start east towards Bloemfontein. This direction of retreat has been criticised,* and

* See summary of a letter of Michael Davitt, whose Boer sympathies are well known, from Kroonstadt, March 31, to the Dublin *Freeman's Journal*, given in the London *Times*, June 25, 1900.

it has been argued that he should have tried to retire to the northward, away from the British divisions already east of him. In this direction a certain proportion of his army did break out. It is to be remembered, however, that not only was Bloemfontein the capital of the Free State, and, therefore, not lightly to be sacrificed, but that his movement was concentric, having regard to Joubert and the bulk of the Boer forces elsewhere. Not only so, but French was north of him; and as it turned out it was French, in virtue of the superior mobility of his cavalry, who headed him off to the eastward, giving time for the British infantry to come up. The trains went with Cronje, and apparently it was his unwillingness to drop them, rather than the direction of his retreat, that lost him. Because men not so encumbered escaped north, it cannot be certainly concluded that he could by the same course have saved his trains.

Be it as it may, Friday morning the 16th found the Boer lines at Magersfontein empty. The presence of British divisions south of the Modder compelled Cronje to take a course north of it. Except for the drifts, the river thus protected his flank; and if he could, by diverging sufficiently, slip undetected past Klip Drift, leaving the easternmost of the British divisions—Kelly-Kenny—in his rear, he might reach the point he aimed at, Koodoosrand Drift, twenty-four miles north-east of Klip Drift, cross there, and so reach the direct road from Jacobsdal to Bloemfontein. This effected, the British would have a stern chase, proverbially long, and in this instance certainly fruitless.

Cronje nearly succeeded. Early on Friday morning the British at Klip Drift saw north of them a great cloud of dust, moving eastward. It was the Boer convoy, in rear of which doubtless was their army. Kitchener sent out mounted infantry to get to the north of the retreating force, while a brigade of foot was directed to keep along the river's bank. Word was sent at once to French in Kimberley, who was employing that day in clearing the country north of the town. The field telegraph being cut by the enemy, he received Kitchener's message late at night. This, after stating Cronje's movements, added that if he, "with all available horses and guns, could head him, and prevent him from crossing the river, the infantry from Klip Drift would press on and annihilate or take the whole force prisoners." *

French left at 3.30 A.M. with one brigade and three batteries, the others to follow as they could with their worn-out animals. The enemy had a long start, but from Kitchener's message it was evident that their march would be steadily harassed and delayed by the frequent necessity of fighting, of resting at times, and by the slow movement of the ox-team. Using utmost speed, at 11 A.M. French's detachment saw the trees lining the Modder's banks, upon which its route had been converging. On the left a fairly large body of men were perceived moving east. A line of hills between these and the British force concealed the latter, who were nearer the river. The horses were ordered to water while the general and staff rode forward to reconnoitre. Reaching a favourable height, they saw, 4,000 yards away, the leading wagons of the Boer convoy just descending

* "The Cavalry Rush to Kimberley," p. 210.

to Koodoosrand Drift, where a road from the northward crosses to Petrusberg, on the Jacobsdal-Bloemfontein highway. The batteries were summoned up, being cautioned to move at a walk, lest their dust should draw attention, and at 12.15 P.M. the first shot was fired which told Cronje that at the very last moment, with safety apparently grasped, his passage was about to be disputed.

The Boer general, who for a day and a half had been fighting a constant succession of rear-guard actions with Kitchener's infantry, took his measures promptly to meet this new dilemma. He first tried to seize positions of command which would give him control of the ford. In this French was the quicker, and headed him. He then turned his column to the right to a ford called Wolveskraal Drift, four miles below, west of Koodoosrand, and the same distance above Paardeberg Drift, from which his defence has received its name. At Wolveskraal he "laagered" his trains on the north bank of the river, postponing crossing to next day. Either he felt sure that the British infantry, marching afoot, could not come up in time to stop him, or else, unable to reconcile himself to cutting loose from his guns and his wagons, he determined to risk all on the chance of saving them. French, unsupported, could only answer for Koodoosrand.

The decision was critical, and proved fatal. The British 6th Division pressed on untiring after nightfall, aiming to reach Paardeberg, but, missing the precise point, they passed on and halted a mile and a half below Wolveskraal, nearly opposite the ford Cronje intended to use. Though all unknowing, they had taken a commanding position to head him, as French had at Koodoosrand. Behind them was the mounted infantry, which had crossed back from the north side, and also the 9th Division. Before daybreak both these had halted on the south side, at Paardeberg.

When Cronje camped on the afternoon of the 17th, the only chance left him was to cross at once to Wolveskraal, abandoning his guns and wagons. On the morning of the 18th no chance was left, except by outside help, which could come only from the eastward, probably only from Joubert before Ladysmith. Realising this, and to gain time for such assistance to arrive, he took up a defensive position based upon the bed of the Modder.

In broad outline his dispositions were as follows. The bed of the river, which lies nearly east and west, is from fifty to one hundred yards wide and about thirty deep, in soil that lends itself easily to the spade. On both sides, for a mile above and below Wolveskraal Drift, the edges of the banks were trenched, and at either end of these trenches traverses, thrown forward at right angles, served to strengthen against enfilading attack. North of the river, some cannon were placed in advanced works, three-quarters of a mile from the rifle pits, between which and the river, in the open, was the "laager" of ammunition and other wagons. The river trenches described constituted the nucleus and backbone of the Boer defences, but in his first dispositions Cronje occupied the bed of the stream down to Paardeberg, seeking thus to push back as far as possible from his intended crossing the force which he supposed had yet to come up from that quarter. The Boers that surrendered numbered 4,100 men. It may be supposed, therefore, that there were from 4,500 to 5,000 present at the first.

South of the river is grassy plain, at its widest 3,000 yards, shelving gently to the bank. Beyond it there is a rise of fifty feet in the ground. Behind this plain, on the morning of Sunday, February 18, the British had in position the 6th Division and of the 9th the 19th Brigade, besides three regiments of Highlanders. The mounted infantry, that had been pursuing the day before on the north bank, now occupied the river-bed west of Cronje's lines. The artillery present was three batteries—two field and one howitzer—with a single naval gun. On the north bank at daybreak was French's cavalry brigade, which was slightly reinforced during the day, and his horse artillery.

Soon after daybreak fighting began, the Boers opening fire at the west end of their line upon the mounted infantry. The latter replying succeeded in driving the enemy a quarter of a mile up stream. While this was occurring the British began a frontal attack in line from the south—the 6th Division on the right, the 9th on the left, the advance of the infantry line being supported by the batteries, placed 2,000 yards south-east of the Boer laager. French's horse artillery also opened from the north bank. As usual in frontal attacks upon a well-entrenched resolute enemy, the loss of the assailants greatly exceeded the results obtained. By an eye-witness the action was likened to Methuens at the Modder.* The fire of the batteries, however, was extremely destructive to the Boer laager, causing several explosions, and great distress to the enemy could not but ensue from this injury to their only base.

The frontal attack was supplemented later by efforts directed upon the flanks. Three regiments—one a Canadian—of the 19th Brigade at 9 A.M. crossed at Paardeberg, and thence fought their way a mile up-stream—east—on the north bank. Here they were stopped, and had to extend their line to the northward; after which, by short and desperate

* London *Weekly Times*, March 23 and April 6 (p. iii). In the absence of official reports other than telegraphic summaries, the author has based his account chiefly on this authority.

rushes, they continued to add by driblets to the ground so far gained. This was strictly a flank attack, and not only shortened by so much the Boer front, but enabled the assailants to enfilade their line in part. The attempt was imitated on the eastern flank by the mounted infantry which, after the arrival of the foot divisions, had moved east from Paardeberg and established themselves on the Boers' eastern flank at Koodoosrand Drift. These crossed at this point at about noon and fought west. An hour later they were supported by the two right — east — regiments of the British line, which by a rush reached the river below Koodoosrand, where a number crossed. These moved west in two parties, in mutual support on either bank.

The frontal attack and the flank movements so far stated summarize the details of this action. Support was sent from time to time as occasion demanded and opportunity offered, especially to the flanking parties. The net result of the day was that Cronje's force, from a development of four miles, was shortened in to two, the British holding the river banks above and below that stretch. with considerable part of their force placed perpendicularly to the river across both the Boer flanks, yet bound together in mutual support by the main body, extended along the southern slope, ready to reinforce in either direction. The flanking parties began immediately to entrench, their lines running, as already intimated, perpendicular to the Boer front, and facing the transverse works which the latter had erected as a protection against enfilading.

The British loss this day is variously estimated from 1,100 to 1,250. The official accounts do not particularise, but give as the total casualties, February 16–27, killed 255, wounded 1,209, missing 70. The propriety of the frontal attack has been much doubted. The question is one of expediency, upon which the author does not presume to give a certain opinion. It may be remembered that the Boer position had been hastily assumed, under conditions not long foreseen, and therefore quite possibly not very solid. The fact could be tested only by trial. So severe an assault unquestionably tends to benumb the victim, and to make less probable his escape, quite independent of his actual loss. Moreover, the flanking gains, which ultimately hastened and determined the inevitable surrender, could scarcely have been secured except under the stress of the frontal attack.

The next day, February 19, Lord Roberts arrived at Paardeberg, and with him the 7th Infantry Division. A reconnaissance, the following afternoon, satisfied him that assault would be attended by very heavy loss. He, therefore, ordered a bombardment, at a range of about 2,000 yards, by between forty-five and fifty guns. Of these, rather more than half were on the northern bank and in enfilading positions. The ground upon which this tremendous fire played was some two miles long by a half-mile wide. The character of the injury is best told by the report of an eye-witness of the conditions. "Nothing could be done but crouch in the trenches and wait till dusk prevented a further attack, while wagon after wagon in the laager caught fire and burned away into a heap of scrap iron surrounded by wood ashes. The desolation produced was fearful, and it soon became impossible to make any reply. The losses inflicted upon the horses were the turning point of the siege. So enormous a proportion (estimated by some at 75 per cent.) of the horses, for which no protection could be made, were lost, that any dash for freedom by night was impossible and the condition of the laager rapidly became so foul, that that alone, apart from the want of food, would have compelled an early surrender. There was no opportunity of getting rid of the vast number of dead animals; burial was impossible, and the low state of the river prevented them from sending them down stream for several days; all they could do was to drag them to leeward of their camp. Meanwhile decomposition set in, and the absolute need of clean air caused a serious rebellion in the camp, most of the 4,000 men demanding that surrender should be made at once. When on Sunday, the 25th, the flood brought down past our lines an unending series of dead animals that cannot have been less than 1,500 or 2,000, the desperate straits of the enemy were apparent indeed."

This benumbing concentrated gun fire of February 20 was not repeated. The British Commander-in-Chief thenceforth satisfied himself with hemming in the enemy, under a steady pressure, the result of which could not be doubtful. A few days more or less were not to be counted against the husbanding of his soldiers' lives, in conditions also of comparative rest, favourable to a recuperation sorely needed by men and horses. The last arrived 7th Division entrenched itself on both sides of the river—a cheval, as the French phrase runs—to the eastward of and perpendicular to Cronje's lines, barring the way against attempts to break out towards Bloemfontein, and against the approach of aid from that quarter. The troops were further occupied by the Boer reinforcements, from Natal, and elsewhere, which began to cluster round the scene, seeking to help the beleaguered army. Several smart actions were fought, but all attempts at relief were vain.

The approach of Majuba Day—February 27 — appears to have influenced both parties, hastening the issue. The Boers, huddled in the narrow and loathsome bed of the river, with senses sickened by the disgusting accumulations of filth and decay inevitable in the circumstances, clamoured for deliverance even at the cost of surrender. Cronje, obstinately bent to prolong to the utmost the chance of succour, is reported to have promised at last to surrender on the 28th, but by no means on the date illustrated by a boasted Boer victory. On the other hand, it is said that Roberts was urged to effect the consummation on that day, in grateful expiation of the disaster that had ever since rankled in British remembrance. One of his brigadiers, Hector MacDonald, now lying wounded, had been present at the earlier humiliation, and recalled the date to the Commander-in-Chief. However it be, a plan was adopted which brought about the desired coincidence. Ever since the 18th, the detachment of which the Canadian Regiment formed part had held the position then gained on the north bank, on the enemy's west flank. There it occupied a trench, running 700 yards north from the river. In the early hours of February 27, long before daybreak, three companies of the

Canadians, acting under specific orders, quitted the trench and moved towards the enemy, followed close at heel by fifty engineer troops. In their silent advance they approached to eighty yards of the Boer traverse trench before discovered. Then a heavy and continuous fire burst forth, lasting for fifteen minutes without intermission. The Canadians lying down replied, while the engineers close behind them dug, till a trench 100 yards long, and giving good cover, ran from the bank to the north. Into it, when finished, the Canadians retired.

The game was won. To quote Roberts' telegram, "At 3 A.M. to-day a most dashing advance made by the Canadian Regiment and some engineers, supported by the 1st Gordon Highlanders and 2nd Shropshires, resulted in our gaining a point some 600 yards nearer the enemy, and within eighty yards of his trenches. This apparently clinched matters." The new position, which passed the power of the Boers to force, enfiladed securely their rifle-trenches along the river, and took in rear the advanced works to the north. At daylight of Majuba

Day, Cronje sent Roberts a letter saying that he surrendered unconditionally.

Briefly summarized, this achievement of the British Army was the dislodgment of an inferior force from an extremely formidable position—at Magersfontein—at the least loss to the victors, by a secret and rapid flank march, followed by a swift pursuit, ending in the enforced surrender of a portion that sought escape in flight. Incidentally, Kimberley was relieved. Such effects, by such use of superior numbers, without which they cannot be accomplished, are always the object of war, which aims not at fighting, but at results. To estimate duly the operation, regard must be had to the impediments to movement, the overcoming of which gave success. The larger force, to compass its object, had to reach secretly and rapidly positions which interposed decisively between the inferior and its line of communications and retreat. To do this secretly, a large circuit must be made; that is, a road must be taken far beyond the enemy's ken, therefore much longer than that he himself would traverse to pass the same decisive points and thereby evade interception. The question is one of exterior and interior lines, and therefore of speed. Speed in a country without resources, and especially when opposed to an enemy notoriously mobile, means not only hard legging and much privation, but very high organisation of transport, to insure even a bare sufficiency of support.

By virtue of the interior line, notwithstanding the rapidity with which Roberts' men and horses moved, Cronje got past the decisive points; but for French he might have escaped. His success in this changed instantly the whole direction of the British operation. Trains directed upon one expectation had to be diverted elsewhere, which means not the mere turning round of waggons, but the reversal of a complicated machinery working at high pressure; perhaps rather the redistribution of parts in an engine while in actual operation. That the transport system under this extreme test stood the strain without dislocation, though with necessarily lessened output, is as creditable as the patient fortitude of the hosts, who lacking full food and water, toiled uncomplainingly in pursuit, under the burning sun, not knowing but that after all their labour would be in vain.

The final, and successful, operations of Sir Redvers Buller for the relief of Ladysmith were almost exactly coincident, in beginning and in duration, with those of Lord Roberts which ended in the surrender of Cronje. There was even a certain close approach to synchronism in dates of the more conspicuous incidents in each.

On the 11th of February, when the departure of French began Roberts' turning movement, Buller's force was again assembled at Chieveley. The following day the direction of his next effort was indicated by the occupation of Hussar Hill, south of Hlangwane Hill, which it will be remembered lies near the Tugela, its crest about three-fourths of a mile east of the bend which the river makes just below Colenso, and after which it holds a northerly course for two or three miles before again running east.

This north and south stretch, as before said, divided the Boer military line of the Tugela. Since the battle of Colenso all their positions had been strengthened, especially the eastern portion south of the river, previously comparatively neglected; and continuous entrenchments now extended from Hlangwane east for three miles to a treeless height named Green Hill. East of this, again, and connected with it, is a range called Monte Cristo, which runs north-west to the Tugela. This district south of the river, and between it and the entrenchments just mentioned, is for the most part rugged and intricate, but less so than the region west of Colenso and north of the stream.

The occupation of Hussar Hill on February 12 was for reconnaissance only. The force was afterwards withdrawn. On the 14th the real movement began. Hussar Hill was again taken, and from that day the operations, though varying in activity, were continuous until the 18th, when, after two days of heavy fighting from hill to hill, the British succeeded in gaining possession of Green Hill, their ultimate object, upon the enemy's left flank. The Boers then evacuated Hlangwane, which was occupied on the 19th by the British. The positions of the Boers south of the Tugela and east of the bend had thus all fallen, weakening their left flank, at the same moment that Roberts, arriving at Paardeberg, found Cronje hemmed in the bed of the Modder.

Buller's turning movement had now driven the Boers into the mountainous country between Colenso and Ladysmith, west of the bend in the Tugela. Here, when his campaign opened in December, had been the strength of their position. Its general character has been already mentioned, as well as some particular features—Grobler's Kloof, two miles above Colenso, the kopjes behind Fort Wylie commanding the bridge, etc. Between Grobler's and the northerly stretch of the river ran the railroad to Ladysmith, threading a maze of hills which a stay of three months had made intimately familiar to the Boers, both men and officers. The accidents of the ground, and their mutual influence from the military point of view, had been carefully studied and artificially improved, by men whose natural aptitudes for defensive warfare and choice of positions is of the highest. In nothing do they seem to have shown more skill than in the preparation of traps, whereby success, won with just sufficient difficulty to seem plausibly brilliant, turns at the very moment of apparent victory into hopeless disaster, entailing either destruction or retreat.

Into this tangle of obstacles the British forces were now about to enter. Colenso, found to be evacuated on February 19, was occupied on the 20th. A reconnaissance pushed across the bridge showed that the kopjes about Fort Wylie, now rendered untenable by the loss of Hlangwane, were but weakly held and their guns gone. On the morning of February 21, the second day after the occupation of Hlangwane, a pontoon bridge was thrown at a point between that hill and Colenso. By midday of the 22nd nearly five brigades of infantry had crossed, and immediately afterwards the advance began. That day and the two following were marked by extremely severe fighting, attended with alternate success and repulse, but the end was failure after very heavy losses. The series of incidents is instructive as a military lesson on warfare in an intricate mountain region; but to follow it would require care and attention, with elaborate maps, and even so would possess sustained interest only for the professional reader.

On the afternoon of February 20, Buller had telegraphed the fall of Hlangwane, adding, "the enemy seem to be in full retreat, and are apparently only holding a position which they occupy across the Colenso-Ladysmith railway, where it is close to the angle of the Tugela, with a weak rear-guard." The mention of the railroad shows that this impression of retreat concerned the enemy west of the bend and north of the river, but it proved to be entirely mistaken. On the 24th of February, it is true, the Boers packed their wagons and moved them north of Ladysmith.* The fact testifies to the vigour of the assault and their consequent anxiety; but in the evening of that same day it had become apparent to the British that the resistance was still so strong that they could not get through by the direction taken, which, speaking generally, was that of the railroad. Sunday the 25th was passed in inaction, removing the wounded

* Buller's telegram from Ladysmith, March 2.

and the dead, and on Monday the whole force was withdrawn across the Tugela at Colenso, to try another movement from further down stream, to the north and east of Hlangwane, and again directed against the enemy's left.

This retreat, though not certainly known, was vaguely suspected in Ladysmith, where the silence of Sunday sounded ominous. The spirits of the now famishing garrison sank accordingly. One among them writes: "The ending has been strange. On Monday, February 26, the garrison was sunk in a slough of despondency. On the previous Thursday General Buller had signalled from below in such confident language that the force had been placed upon full rations. Then, day by day, we had watched for some sign of the promised relief. Daily the guns had boomed, and occasionally we had caught a glimpse of the burst of an 'accidental,' but nothing more. Heavy weather had settled upon us and had blinded the little winking reflector on Monte Cristo Hill. On Sunday the relieving force must have been engaged in a night attack, for the sound of volley firing was distinctly audible in Ladysmith. Then came a day of silence. The helio was veiled in cloud, and there were no sounds of war. The spirits of the garrison fell. Grave rumours circulated. Men even said that for the third time the relief column had recrossed the Tugela. Monday brought a wave of hope, for at midday there was a gleam of sunshine, and we learned the news that Cronje had been surrounded in the Free State. Still there was no news from Buller's column. It was evident that the staff were also becoming anxious, for although the following day brought the news that Cronje had surrendered, yet the evening saw the garrison again reduced to quarter rations. This was only a precautionary measure, for Buller had helioed 'everything progressing favourably.' But the man in the street was sceptical. If favourable, why reduce the ration? Thus it was that Tuesday, Majuba Day—although on that date the tide of fortune had turned in our favour—marked the lowest pitch of despondency into which the garrison was ever plunged during the 118 days of its investment." *

* London *Weekly Times*, March 30, 1900.

The end of their sufferings, however, was really at hand. Buller's telegram of February 28 announcing the success of the next operation, states also its character. "Finding that the passage of Langewachte Spruit (the scene of the fighting on the 23rd and 24th) was commanded by strong entrenchments, I reconnoitred for another passage of the Tugela. One was found for me below the cataract by Colonel Sandbach, Royal Engineers. . . . On the 26th, finding that I could make a practicable approach, I crossed the guns and baggage back to the south side of the Tugela, took up the pontoon bridge on the night of the 26th, and relaid it at the new site. . . . On the 27th General Barton, with two battalions 6th Brigade and the Royal Dublin Fusiliers, crept about one and a half miles down the banks of the river, and, ascending an almost precipitous cliff of about 500 feet, assaulted and carried the top of Pieter's Hill. This hill to a certain extent turned the enemy's left, and the 4th Brigade, under Colonel Norcott, and the 11th Brigade, under Colonel Kitchener, the whole under General Warren, assailed the enemy's main position, which was magnificently carried by the South Lancashire Regiment about sunset."

This handsome operation, which finally loosed the bonds in which Ladysmith was held, should perhaps be described in more detail than a telegram commonly admits. At the lower end of the northerly stretch of the Tugela, below Colenso, where the river again turns east, the railroad, which has kept close to the west bank, also inclines east for a mile and a half, constrained still to cling to the stream by hills to the northward. The more conspicuous of these had been named Terrace Hill and Railway Hill, and there it was that the British attacks of the 24th had been baffled. After passing them the road leaves the river, runs north, and in another mile reaches Pieter's Station. A mile to the eastward of this is Pieter's Hill, which the river nears by a northerly bend in its course. The Boer position north of this section of the river stretched from Railway Hill, three-quarters of a mile west of the road, to Pieter's Hill. The British occupied the heights on the opposite side, between one and two miles distant, and 200 feet above the bed of the Tugela. Along these crests they mounted heavy guns, a sustained fire from which, as is usual, preceded the attack.

On February 27—Majuba Day—as the troops detailed for the assault were about to step on to the bridge, there was communicated to them the news of Cronje's surrender at an earlier hour of the same day, flashed by the wires around from the Modder by way of the sea. Under this inspiring intelligence they went into action. The crossing was made near the angle of the river, where it turns the second time and resumes its easterly direction. Barton's brigade, which was to carry Pieter's Hill—the enemy's left—crossed first, and inclining to the right kept along the river a mile and a half to its appointed place, followed successively by Kitchener's and Norcott's brigades, which thus, when the line was formed, constituted respectively the centre and left of the British front of assault.

The attack on Pieter's was first made, beginning about 1 P.M. By the capture of this the Boer left was turned, after which by assaults progressing successively from the British right to the left, in continuous mutual support, all the works on Railway and Terrace Hills were carried by sunset, the enemy being, in many cases, driven out at the point of the bayonet. The British entrenched themselves that night in their new gains, but next morning, February 28, the Boers were found to have retreated from all the positions from which they had not been expelled. There was no defensive line remaining south of Ladysmith in which they could make a further stand, and the relief of the place followed as a matter of course. An advance party under Lord Dundonald entered the town that evening, and Buller himself followed the next day, March 1.

In these final operations for the relief of Ladysmith, the British loss in the Official Table of Casualties is given under two heads: 1, Monte Cristo, February 15–18, being those on the Boer left, south of the Tugela, ending in the capture of Hlangwane Hill; 2, Relief of Ladysmith, February 19–27. In the first there were: Killed 14, Wounded 188, Missing 4; Total 206. In the second: Killed 263, Wounded 1621, Missing 12; Total 1896. These losses are most suggestive of thought as to the character of the operations in which they were respectively incurred. The second total exceeds considerably that reported for any other action, or series of actions, during the war. Spion Kop, with 1733, is the nearest approach.

The advance of Lord Roberts to Bloemfontein after Cronje's surrender met with little resistance. The first position taken by the Boers to contest his progress appears to have been four or five miles east of Koodoosrand Drift. In his telegram their line is described as extending four miles north and eleven miles south of the Modder, a length which evidently required a pretty large force to man it. Its extremities, however, received no protection from natural obstacles of ground, and on the 7th of March French's Cavalry Division, passing south, turned their left flank. The Boers then retreated without serious fighting, the British having only fifty casualties. Three days later, at Driefontein, between forty and fifty miles from Bloemfontein, a stand was made which required a severe struggle to overcome.

The enemy opposed us throughout yesterday's march," Roberts telegraphed; "and from their intimate knowledge of the country gave us considerable trouble. . . . The brunt of the fighting fell upon Kelly-Kenny's division, two battalions of which, the Welsh and the Essex, turned the Boers out of two strong positions at the point of the bayonet." The British here lost 63 killed, 361 wounded. The defenders, contrary to their habit, failed to carry away their dead, of whom the victors buried 127. In the Boer papers their loss was reported to be seven killed and eighteen wounded—a suggestive discrepancy. No further opposition of consequence was encountered, and on March 13 Roberts entered Bloemfontein.

The occupation of Bloemfontein and the relief of Ladysmith closed for a time the British operations, and were followed by a period of suspended advance. This was imposed in part by the fatigue of the soldiery, a cause, however, which would not have lasted more than a few days—except in the case of the hunger-weakened defenders of Ladysmith. A prolonged stop was required for several reasons. The conduct of the war had now reverted to the original plan of an invasion in force through the Free State by the great mass of the British army. To this, all other movements were subsidiary, including those of even such a great corps as that of Buller, upon a line so important as the Natal railroad. But the central mass under the Commander-in-Chief had momentarily exhausted itself, not in organic vitality but in function power of movement, owing to the excessive strain upon the transport service and the expenditure of animal life in the forced marches and severe privations in the past month under conditions always most trying to unacclimated horses. The British Assistant Secretary of War said in Parliament that Lord Roberts arrived at Bloemfontein with his horses wholly starved and his men half-starved. The "wreck of an army," wrote a correspondent present, "lies scattered in and about Bloemfontein." Paralysing as such a condition is under any circumstances it was trebly so in a force which by a sudden rush, a leap rather than a march, had projected itself a hundred miles from any solid base of operations, and had not yet its communications secured. How much more was this true when a great further advance of 250 miles was intended. In short, before moving forward, it was necessary to insure that the connection behind was established, and the provision for transport ahead adequately developed. This involved not only an immense accumulation of animals, to allow for a waste always extreme, but also large reinforcements of troops; for every step forward in an enemy's country requires a detachment left behind to secure it.

"At each remove the lengthening chain" demands its group of guards, and these wisely disposed for quick mutual assistance; for with any enemy, and especially with one so mobile, it is impossible to be everywhere in sufficient force, superior to an unexpected attack. Communications are ever on the defensive, the most embarrassing of military attitudes. To the scattered units of such a system, all that can be provided is power to hold out until succoured. Moreover, there must be not merely a steady stream of supply from some far distant source, but the establishment of intermediate reservoirs—secondary depôts—well stored with the manifold requirements of an army in campaign ; advanced bases, capable by themselves of supporting for an appreciable time the existence and activity of forces dependent upon them alone. The importance of these to the army make them ever an object of attack to the enemy. Provision against accident or interruption, casual or hostile, has therefore to be elaborate in framework and solid in joint. "Lord Roberts had 45,000 men when he arrived at Bloemfontein, and he increased that number to 75,000 by April 30." Six thousand horses, besides mules, were at the same time sent up. To supply men and animals with daily food, and to accumulate on the spot twenty-five days' provisions and supplies of military stores for the further advance to the Vaal, there had to be brought daily to Bloemfontein, besides the reinforcements of men, 1020 tons by a single-track railroad on which many bridges had been destroyed.* And Bloemfontein was 750 miles from Cape Town, and 250 from De Aar, the nearest secondary base so far established.

* These figures are taken from a speech made by the Under Secretary of War in Parliament, June 29, 1900.

The good effect of Roberts's advance upon the general fortune of the war, and the correct military principle of the original plan, by him resumed, were clearly and quickly evident. Men from the Boer forces before Ladysmith were assembling already around Paardeberg before Cronje surrendered, seeking to relieve him, and Roberts on his march to Bloemfontein fought not only them but others from Colesberg and Stormberg, and generally from the regions over which French and Gatacre had vainly striven to advance. How far this helped Buller in his actual fighting before Ladysmith cannot certainly be said. The comparative ease with which Hlangwane Hill was carried, was probably due chiefly to the correct direction given to the attack, while the heavy loss of the following days, February 22–24, may also be assigned to a frontal assault undertaken under a mistaken impression as to the enemy's force. The Boers did not then fight like men who were merely a rear guard covering a retreat. Nevertheless, there are indications that their numbers had been materially weakened, and the consciousness that Roberts's success would necessitate the abandonment of the siege may have affected the fighting, especially after Cronje's surrender became known.

The effect at Colesberg and in the Stormberg region is less doubtful. The imminence of Roberts's advance, when his purpose became apparent, drew away so many of the enemy to oppose him that the task of Clements and Gatacre became relatively easy and rapid. On March 15, two days after the occupation of Bloemfontein, Clements, whose temporary retirement has been noted, reached and held Norval's Pont, where the line from Naauwport to Bloemfontein crossed the Orange; while Gatacre, so long at a stand-still, the same day occupied Bethulie, where the road from East London bridges the river. These two points are only about thirty miles apart, the converging roads meeting thirty miles beyond, at Springfontein. This junction was occupied next day, March 16, by a brigade sent back by Roberts. By the holding of these points, railroad communication was restored, in a military sense, from Bloemfontein to Cape Town and to East

London. To assure it in practice as well, there was needed only certain repairs, and adequate guards disposed round these central positions.

Coincidently with the forward movement of Clements and Gatacre, a similar advance upon the latter's right flank, and, in a sense, covering it, was made by a colonial division of 2,000 men under a colonial officer, General Brabant. This took its direction to the eastward of the easternmost railway system, midway between it and the Basutoland boundary, traversing the mountainous region in which lay the districts of Cape Colony, Herschel, Aliwal North, etc., that early in the war had been annexed by proclamation of the President of the Free State. After crossing the Orange, this division continued to skirt the Basuto line by Rouxville and Wepener, thus entering the region south and east of Bloemfontein, which shortly became the scene of the enemy's movements threatening Roberts's communications with Cape Colony—movements characterised by a certain daring in conception and execution, but to which the customary caution of the

Boers gave a direction too eccentric to constitute a home-thrust.

From February 11, when Roberts left the Modder, to March 13, when Bloemfontein was occupied, his operations and forward movement had been practically continuous. The subsequent halt, imperative as it was for the reasons stated, gave the Boers breathing time in which to recover themselves. Advance in force by the British main body was not resumed until May 2, but detachments were moved about in various directions on the near front, and on flank and rear, to occupy necessary outposts, to secure the communications, and to insure quiet among the inhabitants. During this prolonged period of recuperation and preparation the enemy resumed activity, scouring the country with their mounted men, seeking to cut off exposed parties, and by menacing the communications, to embarrass and retard the British commander in his new arrangements. In the first of these measures the Boers attained some successes; but in the second, either their numbers were too few for their object, or their habitual caution prevented resort to action in such force and at such risk as is absolutely necessary either seriously to "interrupt" communications—in the military sense of the phrase—or to produce any deterrent impression upon a commander of the experience and sound judgment of the one with whom they were dealing. Not only did they not materially threaten the communications, but it was perfectly evident that, whatever their reasons, they dared not attempt to do so.

As regards the cutting off of British detachments, of which the affairs of Reddersburg and of Koorn Spruit, near Thaba Nchu, were the most conspicuous illustrations, the only thing essential to be remarked is that such reverses on a small scale are always to be expected in war, in even the most successful campaigns. This does not mean that no blame attaches to them. Very probably in most such cases there has been carelessness or miscalculation, for which somebody merits either punishment or censure. But the Commander-in-Chief and the nation concerned have to reckon upon such mishaps; and, without affecting indifference, or neglecting to exact responsibility, they are to be regarded merely as the bruises and the barked limbs that men get in any rough sport. These they are, and usually they are nothing more. The player does not bleed to death in consequence; he simply goes on with the game. Military men, of course, understand this, but nations are too apt to be fretful as though some strange thing had happened to them.

It is not by such affairs that contests are decided—on the playground or in strategy. Lord Roberts proceeded with his preparations undisturbed by the mosquito buzzings about his ears or on his trail. At last, when ready, a second long leap was made. The British army, leaving Bloemfontein on the 2nd of May, was on the 12th at Kroonstad, over 100 miles distant. On the 24th the Vaal was crossed, and on the 31st Roberts entered Johannesburg. Five days later, on the 5th of June, the British flag was hoisted in Pretoria, the capital of the Transvaal, 250 miles from Bloemfontein. The sustained momentum of this advance, achieved in very little over a month, testifies at once to the solidity oi the preparations of the British leader, and to the fruitlessness of such disseminated operations, by small bodies, as were conducted by the Boers during the British halt at Bloemfontein, and are now being carried on by Botha and De Wet. Subsidiary to the greater plan of a campaign by massed forces, they have their advantage; as a main dependence, they merely protract the agony of endurance and suffering.

Sir Redvers Buller had to await in Natal the movement of the central mass of the British force in the Orange Free State. Towards the middle of May his advance began, directed against the positions which the Boers had taken upon the Biggarsberg mountains, and on the 15th he re-occupied Dundee and Glencoe. Into the detail of these movements it is not proposed to enter. The retirement of the Boer forces before Roberts, in the Free State, uncovered the flank and endangered the communications of their brethren on the other side of the mountains. There was therefore for these nothing to do but to fall back, abandoning with a show of opposition positions whence otherwise they might have inflicted considerable loss upon the superior force assaulting them.

At the present moment, July 26, the British have communication from Johannesburg and Pretoria to the sea-coast by two routes—to Cape Town and to Durban. The actions of the Boers show that it is not in their power seriously to incommode either the one or the other. The trivial raids performed by their mounted men under De Wet and Botha may protract the sufferings of the war, and add to the close of the struggle a certain lustre of persistent resistance; but, barring events now unforeseen and scarcely to be anticipated, they cannot change the issue, which has become simply a question of endurance between combatants immeasurably unequal in resources.

HOW WRONG THIS FINAL ANALYSIS IS.

INDEX